T0346697

WILLIAM JAMES

My Reading

PHILIP DAVIS

WILLIAM JAMES

OXFORD

UNIVERSITY PRESS

OXFORD
UNIVERSITY PRESS

Great Clarendon Street, Oxford, OX2 6DP,
United Kingdom

Oxford University Press is a department of the University of Oxford.
It furthers the University's objective of excellence in research, scholarship,
and education by publishing worldwide. Oxford is a registered trade mark of
Oxford University Press in the UK and in certain other countries

© Philip Davis 2022

The moral rights of the author have been asserted

First Edition published in 2022
Impression: 1

Published in the United States of America by Oxford University Press
198 Madison Avenue, New York, NY 10016, United States of America

British Library Cataloguing in Publication Data
Data available

Library of Congress Control Number: 2021953532

ISBN 978–0–19–284732–4

DOI: 10.1093/oso/9780192847324.001.0001

Printed and bound in the UK by
Clays Ltd, Elcograf S.p.A.

SERIES INTRODUCTION

This series is built on a simple presupposition: that it helps to have a book recommended and discussed by someone who cares for it. Books are not purely self-sufficient: they need people and they need to get to what is personal within them.

The people we have been seeking as contributors to *My Reading* are readers who are also writers: novelists and poets; literary critics, outside as well as inside universities, but also thinkers from other disciplines—philosophy, psychology, science, theology, and sociology—beside the literary; and, not least of all, intense readers whose first profession is not writing itself but, for example, medicine, or law, or a non-verbal form of art. Of all of them we have asked: what books or authors feel as though they are deeply *yours*, influencing or challenging your life and work, most deserving of rescue and attention, or demanding of feeling and use?

What is it like to love this book? What is it like to have a thought or idea or doubt or memory, not cold and in abstract, but live in the very act of reading? What is it like to feel, long after, that this writer is a vital part of your life? We ask our authors to respond to such bold questions by writing not conventionally but personally—whatever 'personal' might mean, whatever form or style it might take, for them as individuals. This does not mean overt confession at the expense of a chosen book or author; but nor should our writers be afraid of making autobiographical connections. What was wanted was whatever made for their own hardest thinking in careful relation to quoted sources and specifics. The work was to go on in the taut and resonant space between these readers and their chosen books. And the interest within that area begins precisely when it is no longer clear how much is coming from the text, and how much is coming from its readers—where that distinction is no longer easily tenable because neither is sacrificed to the other. That would show what reading meant at its most serious and how it might have relation to an individual life.

Out of what we hope will be an ongoing variety of books and readers, *My Reading* offers personal models of what it is like to care about particular authors, to recreate through specific examples imaginative versions of what those authors and works represent, and to show their effect upon a reader's own thinking and development.

ANNE CHENG

PHILIP DAVIS

JACQUELINE NORTON

MARINA WARNER

MICHAEL WOOD

For the Students and Readers, over the Years:
'Live all you can; it's a mistake not to.'

PREFACE

Who Was He?

William James (1842–1910) was elder brother to the novelist Henry James; New York born, Harvard professor, a founder of the study of psychology. But he was also a thinker who sought to work across conventional boundaries, and did not believe in separate disciplines or over-professionalized ways of thinking.

What Did He Write?

His first major work, *The Principles of Psychology*, a great textbook of 1400 pages, was twelve years in the making, and finally appeared in 1890 when James was forty-eight. Subsequent works were mainly made up of collected essays and lectures. Especially important in this present book are *The Will to Believe and Other Essays* (1897), *The Varieties of Religious Experience* (1902), *Pragmatism* (1907), *A Pluralistic Universe* (1908), and *The Meaning of Truth* (1909).

What Was His Philosophy?

It had sundry names, none of which James himself much cared for. It is best described as 'process philosophy', involving the dynamic processes of time and continuous change, or as 'American pragmatism'. But pragmatism here is not as we think of it in relation to certain politicians being 'pragmatic': wily and cynical, working craftily within the easy limits of what is possible and expedient. It is rather to do with widening the range of what is possible, trying out what may work, finding what is useful to human beings in the midst of things, without absolute principles or goals set up in advance. Other names James used to describe his adventure in thinking included 'humanism', that humans have a vote in life, are in the game and not mere on-lookers; 'radical empiricism', that reality consists not only in single down-to-earth specifics but also in our experience of the relations between them; and 'pluralism', that there are many varied ways to think, and not just one.

My Reading: William James is not a technical account of the development of William James's philosophy, though ever increasingly James moved away from a sense of dualism, from thinking that the mental and the physical are separate, or that there is a strict border between the mind inside and the world outside. Nor is it written by a philosopher, offering an abstract summary of James's philosophical theories. It is about the personal experience of reading William James, where reading means being involved in the very movement of his sentences, suddenly creating ideas to work with. That means extensive quotation from James's work, particularly those places where thoughts are 'hot' and 'alive', as he put it. I am a reader of literature above all, but one who feels he needs, even in that, the help of psychology and philosophy, to get the thinking out, and into a life. It is William James's life-writing, writing for the sake of existence, that helps me put together literature, psychology, and philosophy, as an amalgam in search of purpose.

How Is This Book Put Together?

James said that religion was created out of the human cry, 'Help! Help!' This book is structured in relation to that idea of 'help!', in a series of experiences of mental obstacles and difficulties—intellectual, psychological, and experiential.

Chapter 1, 'I am a motor', is about the start—James's own delayed beginnings and his recurring problems with depression, but also the kick-start that James's thinking provides for his reader.

Chapter 2 is about learning to read William James, his language, his grammar, and its relation to a radical world-view. Together these two initial chapters try to show why I think of William James as a 'literary' thinker, in whom you can see thought not finished and aloof, but in the very act of its making.

Chapters 3 and 4 then take this crucial language into particular human case-histories: these chapters are, so to speak, 'James, not Pure, but Applied' or as he himself would have dared to put it, 'James Cashed In'. Chapter 3 is about the need to believe and the risk of believing, in relation to modern-day doubts and dispersals. Chapter 4 concerns James's idea of a field of consciousness, a moving and shifting sense of exploratory experience beyond the restrictive ideas of a 'self'.

But Chapter 5 is a counter-chapter, offering challenges and objections to William James's brave and exhilarating view, partly through the story of his student W. E. B. Du Bois, who became a great African-American activist, and partly through the problems of belief, hope, and feeling embodied in the work and person of Thomas Hardy.

Chapter 6 brings the story to an end in terms of James's continuing belief in life and thought and feeling as essentially *dramatic* in their happening, and my sense of the value of that way of being.

Who Is This Book For?

Anyone who has experienced the personal need for thinking and feels the excitement of ideas. That means not only finding thoughts that get you somewhere, but seeking a different way of thinking to make a life more alive. It is for readers, especially readers of literature, who might favour my attempt to create, like William James, a literary way of thinking *outside* the realm of literature.

Philip Davis

With particular thanks to these readers: Rosemarie Bodenheimer, David Constantine, Alison Liebling, Bruce Mangan, and Salley Vickers, and as ever, Jacqueline Norton at OUP.

CONTENTS

1

THE *START*

'I Am a Motor'

' A motor' is what William James called himself, and that is what he is in this book: a human motor force, performing in his readers the equivalent of the work of the spinal cord and the brain's motor cortex, to create movement—mental, emotional, and physical. William James stands for the intellectual and psychological transformation of neurological driving forces into fully human thought and action. He gets under the skin, inside the very nerves of live thinking.

His father, Henry James senior (1811–82), wasn't a motor. At thirteen he had been badly burned trying to stamp out a fire in a barn and had to have a leg amputated. The son of a self-made man from Ireland who amassed a million-dollar fortune in real estate in New York, Henry inherited sufficient wealth to be free to do whatever he wanted. It was not to be his father's business. In reaction against his father's narrow and severe puritanism, he became an independent religious and ethical thinker, an unorthodox mystic visionary. Writer of numerous eccentric works on the liberating reform of morality and religion for a modern world, he would take every opportunity to give strange, vigorous talks, far and wide. But as his wife wrote to Henry junior the novelist, the philosopher-father would return home 'rather discouraged, I think, as he always is, after giving a lecture'. He poured out his heart, and nothing came back but silence. It disappointed and depressed him, this gap between the intense thoughts he had in him and the indifference of the world outside:

> All that he has to say seems so good and glorious, and easily under-
> stood to him, but it falls so dead upon the dull or sceptical ears who
> come to hear him, that I do not wonder that he feels so.[1]

'It falls so dead.' Nearly thirty years later in the ninth lecture of *The Varieties of Religious Experience* (1902), William James was to write one of his most vital sentences: 'All we know is that there are dead feelings, dead ideas, and cold beliefs, and there are hot and live ones.'[2] As a youth, William had once sketched a wry and rueful frontispiece for his father's work, a man flogging a dead horse. Actually, he loved the way that the experience of thinking in his father was 'something realized at a stroke, and felt like a fire in his breast'. But all attempts at the articulation of *what* exactly he believed were 'makeshifts of a more or less desperately impotent kind'.[3]

Whatever his own fate, the father spared nothing in the desire that his children, four boys and a girl, should *be* something—whatever they wanted. And yet with all the resources of a liberal education and extensive travel throughout Europe, the very free-dom made it burdensomely less clear what specifically to choose to do. Henry junior was good at distancing himself from his father's expectations, William the eldest son much less so. Apart from a few promising articles in philosophic journals, the first publication by William was a posthumously edited collection of his father's 'literary remains' in 1885—an act of love and loyalty in attempted reparation for external neglect, by a man aged forty-three. Intensely intelligent, warm, and talented in multiple directions, William James had tried to be a painter in his twenties, then at Harvard had turned instead to science, to physiology, and to medicine, seeking some right field for action that seemed a true fit for him rather than a narrowing. But he disliked institutions and academic boundaries, was easily bored, and often impatient.

It was the raw beginnings he loved: as soon as ideas and courses became established and accepted, he felt them turn secondary and dead. By 1874, in his thirties, he was teaching psychology at Harvard, still in its rudimentary beginnings as a subject, on the back of his training in physiology. He was struggling to bring body and brain into relation with mind, to follow nerves into the creation of personality. In 1878 he was finally commissioned to write a great textbook on the principles of psychology. But it seemed he might never finish it, and it was twelve years before it came out.

In a letter to his older brother in October 1885, Henry junior wrote of his own fears for the reception of his novel, *The Bostonians*. Even so, how can one murmur about one's success not being all one would one like, he wrote, 'when one thinks of the pathetic, tragic ineffectualness of poor Father's lifelong effort, & the silence and the oblivion that seems to have swallowed it up?' Yet William James wasn't going to be ineffectual, for all the weight of anxious depression and sexual frustration, and the illnesses of back and stomach and head and eyes, which he bore in the late 1860s and early 1870s. In those years he felt he had no vocation, and at the worst times no real connection with the world outside. As he was put it more generally in *The Principles of Psychology*:

Whatever things have intimate and continuous connection with my life are things of whose reality I cannot doubt. Whatever things fail to establish this connection are things which are practically no better for me than if they existed not at all.[4]

In melancholy the objects seen or heard did not reach the person. The sufferer was not in touch and could not be affected. It was as though a glass wall separated the depressive from all sense of reality. Quoting the German neurologist and psychiatrist, Wilhelm Griesinger, James wrote how joy made the world seem alive, warm, and near, and made whoever could feel it young again; but depression aged and killed. 'All we know is that there are dead feelings, dead ideas, and cold beliefs, and there are hot and live ones.' But at times in his late twenties, for a young man feeling old, it had been even worse than deadness, closer to madness, and suicide. The death in March 1870 of his young cousin, Minny Temple, the most free and brave and lively person he had ever known, left William at rock bottom. Henry loved her too: hers was, he said, the death of both the brothers' youth. Under cover, William later wrote of his case in the lecture on 'The Sick Soul' in *The Varieties of Religious Experience* where a man, in horrible fear of his own existence, recalls the terrifying image of an epileptic patient he had seen in an asylum. Remembering him motionless all day, with black lifeless eyes, skin almost green, the asylum visitor suddenly now thought, *'That shape am I*…potentially' (VRE, p. 128). James said it was a case-history translated from the French, but it described himself in 1870 after Minny Temple's death. 'Shape' was often how he felt his experience. Within its enclosure, the tiniest of hesitancies offered by 'potentially' was all he had to work with.

It was from within just such a physical and mental predicament that the psychological origins of the *need* for religion came to

William James. Out of existential crisis came the repeated one-word cry that no one on earth seemed to answer: 'Help! Help!' Looking for help, James could not understand how other people around him could go on so obliviously. Why didn't *they* feel the radical insecurity which had turned everything solid in himself to a quivering mass? As a result of that terrible sense of asymmetry, he kept from his people how bad it was, especially from his cheerfully unaware mother, Mary.

What the new psychology of William James was to offer was help. But it worked not as it was to in Freud, by making psychology primarily the study of mental illness. Psychology in James was about amassing the vital conditions for living well, for the right working of mental life in the ability to feel and act and create. As he was to put it at the end of his lecture 'Is Life Worth Living?':

> These then are my last words to you: Be not afraid of life. Believe that life is worth living, and your belief will help create the fact.

'Help! Help!' was turned into 'belief will help…create'. Even in his own trouble during the years of frustration, the potential was always that the unformed mess and waste might shape itself into some new amalgam, become a rich hybrid form of art and science, of physiology, psychology, and philosophy. Dirt, James was to say in lecture 6 in *The Varieties of Religious Experience* on 'the sick soul', was only 'matter out of place' (p. 108).[5] Moved into its right place or seen in its real light, it might be rescued from neglect and misuse. Mobility, as against stuckness, was always the key, an '*unstiffening*' of set concepts and positions and boundaries, of opinions and arguments. It was a term James took rather late in the day from an Italian follower of his, Giovanni Papini: thinking can free and loosen. Here I am, he wrote Papini in 1906, in my 60s, still taking careful steps along the way—but *you*, 40 years my junior:

> you with a pair of bold strides get out in a moment beyond the pathway altogether into the freedom of the whole system, — into the open country. It is your temper of *carelessness*, quite as much as your particular formulas, that has had such an emancipating effect on my intelligence.   (Perry, p. 314)

That is what James admired in what he called genius, a radical carelessness whatever the field: faith in religion, courage in action, daring in thought were all analogous versions of each other. A genius was one who moved into a world that as a result of the movement itself became more 'unfenced, uncultivated, untidy, and unpredictable – a world which slipped through every ideal container, and resisted the impression of every logical mould' (Perry, p. 330). That was what was wanted: a breakthrough to blow open the walls of rigidified systems.

Otherwise, back in the 1870s James had feared he was becoming just another of those middle-aged men who had made 'one blunder after another, and still lies in middle life at the foot of the hill'. That was where James, reading a dramatized version of a son's redundancy in *Hamlet*, feared himself to be, at the bottom of the pile: 'liable to grow sicklied o'er with self-distrust, and to shrink from trials with which his powers can really cope' (*PP* 1, pp. 306–7, chapter 10, 'Consciousness of Self'). If only that outside perception of *'really* cope' could be internalized within that self-belittling *'shrink'* and transformed into a confidence worthy of the discouraged potential. It was as if he was sometimes writing to that earlier self.

'Believe that life *is* worth living, and your belief will help create the fact' is another of James's great sentences, however hard to turn into practice. But that was what he lived for—the moment when the content of life began to take form not as an end but as a direction, through which to develop a future in the making. The key was intuitively to sense an opportunity just ahead, an opening, a chance, and whatever it was, make it become *you* in action, or make yourself become *it* embodied, charging it with the force of your need and your past and your very being. 'Every time a resolve or a fine glow of feeling evaporates without bearing practical fruit is worse than a chance lost; it works so as positively to hinder future resolutions and emotions from taking the normal path of discharge' (*PP* 1, p. 125, chapter 4, 'Habit'). This he wrote ruefully, again from his own experience. By not turning thinking quickly into doing, we mar ourselves. 'Could the young but realize how soon they will become mere walking bundles of habits, they would give more heed to their conduct while in the plastic state' (*PP* 1, p. 127, ibid.). He was thirty-six in 1878 when he married Alice, who felt that she had taken on what the death of Minny Temple had broken. In the same year he signed the contract for his book on psychology. He was forty-eight when the *Principles* finally come out: he had by then just about learnt how to think and live by them. It was his second life, productive now of lecture after lecture, book after book.

But in using his own autobiography, William James is not a novelist as his more famous brother was. His reader is not always given the particular situation in life out of which a thought arises. His thought is more like a line of poetry looking for a host to pick up its resonant applicability, a reader to supply a mental home for its meaning and a context for its completion. Action was simpler in the old external world of physical crisis—dramatic examples were easier to find or imagine:

We stand on a mountain pass in the midst of whirling snow and blinding mist, through which we get glimpses now and then of paths which may be delusive. If we stand still, we shall be frozen to death. If we take the wrong road, we shall be dashed to pieces. We do not certainly know whether there is any right one. What must we do?   ('The Will to Believe')

But even that was not so simple, as the inner grammar reveals:

1. *shall be* frozen, *shall be* dashed to pieces /
2. *may* be delusive, do *not certainly* know, *any* right road /
3. what *must* we do...

In James's nervous system of linguistic shorthand, the depressive 'I can't' was answered by we *must* trust a *may*.

In the world of abstract thought, without that freezing mist and snow, it would be entirely possible to stand still. There you often did not have to decide or do anything. There it could be good not be pressurized into decision, just for the sake of psychological relief. And in that theoretic world it could be argued that we have positively no right to believe anything as true, without the grounds of sufficient evidence. For a formal philosopher, true thinking was the work of Reason, of Logic, of Mind, discovering Truths and Laws that existed like eternal and universal verities prior to, and independent of, humans knowing them. But in James's lexicon there are no capital letters—Reason, Logic, Mind, A Priori Truths or Eternal Laws—however noble their conception:

Both theoretically and practically this power of framing abstract concepts is one of the sublimest of our human prerogatives. We come back into the concrete from our journey into abstractions, with an increase both of vision and of power. It is no wonder that earlier thinkers, forgetting that concepts are only man-made extracts from the temporal flux, should have ended by treating them as a superior type of being, bright, changeless, true, divine, and utterly opposed in nature to the turbid, restless lower world.

(A Pluralistic Universe, lecture 5,
'The Compounding of Consciousness')

But it is the old story, James says, that what started as a wonderfully useful and necessary practice to make life more comprehensible and foreseeable, hardens into a set method, and then a stuck habit, until finally it becomes a tyranny defeating the very end it was used for. Too often we don't 'come back' from our journey into abstractions, to dissolve our concepts back down again into action within the daily world. Then we are left with what James called 'vicious intellectualism' (A Pluralistic Universe, lecture 2, 'Monistic Idealism'). His opponents would argue that James was not a genuine philosopher: that his practicality was the desperate shortcut for a man who felt he had lost too many years vacillating between possibilities. Pure Reason said that not to be *for* something was not necessarily to be against it. But James replied, 'Of course this is a safe enough position *in abstracto*. . . . But, unfortunately, neutrality is not only inwardly difficult, it is also outwardly unrealizable, where our relations to an alternative are practical and vital' ('Is Life Worth Living?'). There come crucial moments when doubting, or refusing to believe that a certain thing *is*, becomes not as pure and neutral as it supposes, but effectively tips over into acting 'as if it were *not*' ('Is Life Worth Living?'). There are still critical occasions in life, James says, when not to decide is itself a decision, when inaction counts as a kind of action, even that of withdrawal.

We may not be in the extreme of simple physical crisis at a mountain pass. But that is where thinking began, as a human response to communications from the world, good and bad. And this is still what thinking now was psychologically: an existential version of the finding of a way in the mist or dark. Thinking in James's world has its origins in being no more and no less than a *middle* department in the flowing structure of the nervous system:

> a mere middle term interposed between an incoming sensation that arouses it and an outgoing discharge…to which itself gives rise. The sensory impression exists only for the sake of awaking the central process of reflection, and the central process of reflection exists only for the sake of calling forth the final act. All action is thus re-action upon the outer word.…The current of life which runs in at our eyes or ears is meant to run out at our hands, feet, or lips.   ('Reflex Action and Theism')

The power of reflective thinking between the incoming and the outgoing exists humanly to modify what otherwise would be only an animal mechanism made out of automatic stimulus and response. But for all the vast amount of mental activity created over and above its immediate use by a hyper-enlarged human brain, the basic early drive towards a practical outcome in life was still 'only postponed, not effaced' ('The Sentiment of Rationality'). 'Cognition, in this view, is but a fleeting moment, a cross-section at a certain point, of what in its totality is a motor phenomenon' ('The Sentiment of Rationality'). That fast moment of inner reflection, in the midst of the overwhelming deluge of everything coming at us from without, gives just sufficient postponement-time for choosing this course, for rejecting that one, for making rapid selection, not out of the leisureliness of dispassionate inquiry but from need and bias and economy. Thinking pulls the switches to excite or to inhibit, to manage the power-surge, to shift and blend it with other nervous forces. It is the beginning of the inner self, the person in the thick of things. And its work began as a further aid to Darwinian survival: to select, to conceive, to foresee. You could delay longer between incoming and outgoing before the release. But thinking remains first of all practical—in an original, urgent, and dynamic sense: it must try to *do* something, it must be *for* the sake of life. And that is what James still wanted—the motor phenomenon in a modern world. The sheer experience of life, he said, 'makes me contemptuous of rationalistic attempts to substitute thin logical formulas for it....I am a motor, need change, and get very quickly bored.'[6] For James, the renewed memory that biologically thinking was meant to be practical, to have an end and an action and an effect in view, was not a reduction but a relief. Thinking was not as idle or useless or remote as his father's audiences too often supposed the thoughts of Henry James senior to be.

But the son also knew that thought would not always find a fit, a place, an action within the world. And if not, then it could hardly survive—not without some way of still holding onto it, stored against the odds. His fellow-psychologist F. W. H. Myers spoke of feelings and thoughts that were made subliminal, retained beneath the level of consciousness, because they were not immediately useful but might become so. Hence the unconscious or the subconscious. If out of that store of all the messy experience he had had, William James could sense some use for it, some occasion for it, some opening just ahead, it was vital to take it quickly, release its energy, and unsystematically follow its promptings. This was a *horizontal* movement, it was not truth from above but en route and ahead. James thinks as he goes along, forward: for him everything is more like a verb than a noun, is really like a gerund caught '*in the making*', '*in the doing*', with active participles made into on-going processes. That is why the philosopher A. N. Whitehead thought

James was as revolutionary as was Galileo when he allegedly said of the earth that it was not the static centre of the universe: *It moves!* James does not believe in Mind as a separate and static presiding centre, an unmoved higher faculty offering disembodied and dispassionate objectivity from above. No, it moves, it is a function and not an entity, and at its best is not cool or cold or loftily impartial, but warm and excited and implicated.

And subtle too, because it is not like a clunky movement from one state to another. It is the barely detectable passage of transition in between the two solid states that matters most. Something happened; a difference was sensed and got made even as you went along. All you know is that, in retrospect, you were in (say) a poor state and sort of stuck, though you might hardly have known to call it that, and then suddenly for a moment got into some new clearing that, equally, felt as if it had been needed without your previously knowing it. Clearly there is now a great emotional difference between the departure point and the arrival point. But there are no wholly separate segments. James might call the two states a and b or x and y: he likes a sort of algebra to describe the not-yet-named, as it is sensed in its nerve-like movement of transition in the dark—here from initial state 'm' to a different state 'n':

> in addition to its being felt at the brief instant of transition, the difference also feels as if incorporated and taken up into the second term, which feels 'different-from-the-first' even while it lasts. It is obvious that the 'second term' of the mind is not bald n, but a very complex object; and the sequence is not simply first '*m*', then '*difference*', then '*n*'; but first '*m*', then '*difference*', then '*n-different-from-m*'.
>
> (PP 1, p. 498, chapter 13, 'Discrimination and Comparison')

It is a psychological version of x-ray vision, of sub-atomic physics, beneath the commonplace chunks and surfaces of experience.

Yet still at any moment in that forward-reaching process you could miss your way, the instinctively felt 'yes' becoming a sudden 'no', the potential for life lost. If you could bear to register it, you could feel the movement even in the ebbs and flows of a serious conversation, its turns to or from some central concern or mutual closeness. But it most reminded James of the art he had once practised:

> Every painter can tell us how each added line deflects his picture in a certain sense. Whatever lines follow must be built on those first laid down. Every author who starts to rewrite a piece of work knows how impossible it becomes to use any of the first-written pages again. The new beginning has already excluded the possibility of those earlier phrases and transitions, while it has at the same time created the possibility of an indefinite set of new ones, no one of which, however, is completely determined in advance. Just so the social surroundings of the past and present hour exclude the possibility of accepting certain contributions from individuals; but they do not positively define what contributions shall be accepted, for in themselves they are powerless to fix what the nature of the individual offerings shall be.
>
> ('Great Men and their Environment')

In that tight room for manoeuvre, there was always the risk that the trail could close up and peter out, go dead and lead nowhere. If the thought he was tracking led only to the re-enforcement of old habitual pathways and the repetition of over-familiar concepts, then James felt himself bored, de-energized, and trapped. He had to stop, unstiffen the terms grown fossilized, and try to start again, in order to be properly creative. This was how James's long depression in the late 1860s and early 1870s remained with him ever after as a fear of becoming blocked and imprisoned in repetitive and predictable pathways of mind. There was always in him an underlying sadness in the fight against depression, said his friend and student John Jay Chapman: 'You felt he had just stepped out of this sadness in order to meet you and was to go back into it the moment you left him.'[7]

What James wanted from his writing was the fight for a second life, as befitted what in lecture 4 of *The Varieties of Religious Experience* he was to call—after Francis Newman—'twice-born souls' (*VRE*, p. 69). They were those who have to begin again after going wrong or getting nowhere. Through sorrows and troubles, deaths and losses, by error and conflict, says Newman in *The Soul* (1847), there may be a second chance for those who were not at home or at ease in existence in the first place, from the very start, but have to *make* something of themselves.

For that twice-born soul, it is not the simple evangelical halleluiah of the born-again. The twice-born retain their wary experience of uncertain struggle at almost every step. Of the continuing risk of being mistaken or deluded, James says to the cautious rationalists, 'For my own part, I have also a horror of being duped; but I can believe that worse things than being duped may happen to a man in this world.' There is no escaping vulnerability to the risk of going wrong again. But then James, the great sentence-maker, adds in the name of health:

> Our errors are surely not such awfully solemn things. In a world where we are so certain to incur them in spite of all our caution, a certain lightness of heart seems healthier than this excessive nervousness on their behalf.   ('The Will to Believe')

The chase for even an iota of truth has more natural priority than the avoidance of all and any error: better to risk being wrong than never risk being right. And for James this exuberant new-world brio, trying for fearlessness, was fuelled by something more than tough nerve and strong will. It was the desire for decisive accomplishment. The emergence of the decisive moment, poised on its own risk, is most characteristically for him not a crude surrender or a regrettable necessity, but the creation of something individually beautiful and almost unique:

> Decisions, for him who makes them, are altogether peculiar psychic facts. Self-luminous and self-justifying at the living moment at which they occur, they appeal to no outside moment to put its stamp upon them or make them continuous with the rest of nature. Themselves it is rather who seem to make nature continuous; and in their rich and intense function of granting consent to one possibility and withholding it from another, to transform an equivocal and double future into an unalterable and simple past.
>
> ('The Dilemma of Determinism')

This is not the dull grammar or reductive vocabulary of someone simply 'making up their mind' or 'taking a punt'. It is less like control than adventure. 'They', the moments 'themselves', decisively cohere as a result of some human individual's initial act of 'granting consent to one possibility and withholding it from another': all that seems needed is the inserted intention intuitively to select the chance and set moving whatever then follows from it. It is as though every form of potential coming into reality might be like that, however apparently small—a decision, an event, an act of faith, an individual reality newly made in the world. For James consciousness is best itself when it bursts out, happens, being almost physically *impulsive*.

That moment needs to be cherished and worked for and sustained. The poet Robert Frost said William James was the best teacher he 'never' had at Harvard. It was reading James's works, not attending the man's classes, that inspired him. 'Every poem', he wrote in his essay 'The Constant Symbol', 'is an epitome of the great predicament; a figure of the will braving alien entanglements.'[8] The opening words are the work of a poet reacting with resolute effort upon the world, the initial thrust of mind into matter. And only then can the poem's possibilities open out, as the first effort gives way to the sheer unfolding process that the initial energies have set in motion. 'Its most precious quality' is then, says Frost, that the poem will have been able to let itself go and find its own way, in the accomplishment of 'its having run itself and carried the poet with it'. This is Frost's version in his own work of James's great predicament, the problem of getting the inkling of a good action or wise inclination to stay in the mind, and find its way forward, amidst competing fears and doubts, temptations and distractions. The strong willed are those who hear that still small voice against the hubbub of surrounding images, and increase its effect by deliberately clinging to it, affirming its thought against the odds:

> Sustained in this way by a resolute effort of attention, the difficult object erelong begins to call up its own congerers and associates and ends by changing the disposition of the man's consciousness altogether. And with his consciousness, his action changes, for the new object, once stably in possession of the field of his thoughts, infallibly produces its own motor effects. The difficulty lies in the gaining possession of that field.   (PP 2, p. 564, chapter 26, 'Will')

This is the breakthrough achievement of getting matter into its right place and shape, of working the motor energy into harnessing the most dynamic use of itself. For then by a kind of loop-back and re-entry system, the process begins to help itself, almost recreating within itself the thinker who began its creation. Then suddenly, Frost at a turn in the midst of his poem finds his own words coming back to help carry him forward, in the ongoing interchange between poem and poet. Or William James, in the middle of difficulty, so positions a thought that it takes over and takes off, calling up from him its own helpful associations, to become its own new action.

I will say more in Chapter 2 of how this is a different feel with a different language, for what becomes a more dynamic world-view. But this is why in some of the lectures and essays that formed the volume *The Will to Believe* (1897) and some of the chapters that had comprised *The Principles of Psychology* (1890), A. N. Whitehead detected the germs of a new period in human thinking. There were other influences, C. S. Peirce and John Dewey who were better systematizers, more formal philosophers of process, Whitehead acknowledged; but it was William James in his speed, impatience, and carelessness who was the instigator. In every sense he was the 'start'—the shock and the onset—that offered the first emergent signs of what it might mean to begin to move to a differently configured sense of the world and its possibilities. That is what James himself went to in Luther, in Bunyan, in Tolstoy in *The Varieties of Religious Experience*: original movements from individual geniuses, from primitive oaks of human life who held within them the very root of the matter from which everything else grew (VRE, p. 147, lecture 8, 'The Divided Self'). James was the motor. And for most of us, people who need to think but are not philosophers, a thoroughly developed system of secondary explanations and abstract representations won't work: what is needed to turn passive to active is something that says implicitly in the very nerves of its thinking what might seem naïve if made explicit: 'Life! Here! This! Now!: Follow it. Develop its future, carry on with "the more" that it signals.' And this has to be felt, trusted, and risked, personally and individually along the line. Not because the personal is wholly and invariably trustworthy. But on the contrary, because it is only the personal that can feel deep inside how bad it is to go wrong, how needful to get more right again. It is only the personal that stakes everything in its take on reality—and, with James, can't help having to reappraise that reality, testing both it and itself, even whilst going on.

*

I shall be re-telling parts of the introductory story I have just sketched in different ways, from different angles and with different applications, in the chapters that follow. That is partly because again and again even in writing this swift initial account in one direction, I have wanted to stop over this idea, that formulation, to ensure that what is suddenly exciting in it does not go past without sufficient realization for its own right—even though the suddenness and the transience are conditions for the power of realization. But this desire to pause and make the connection is related to how these thoughts are meant to be useful and to be used as 'help, help'. Because whatever is offered here via William James is to be taken as applied thinking, to be embodied as consequences in actual lives.

His thinking never looked to be pure or abstract. As he dared to put it, it had always to be 'cashed in', to see what it amounted to. It is not that James doesn't believe in what he calls 'pure' experience. But pure experience is primordially dumb and unfocused, chaotic, and undifferentiated in its sensations—at its most absolute the sort of immediate experience, in full and continuous streaming, that James famously ascribes to babies who 'assailed by eyes, ears, nose, skin and entrails at once' feel it all 'as one great blooming buzzing confusion' (*PP* 1, p. 488, chapter 13, 'Discrimination and Comparison'). In his astonishing shorthand for the pre-verbal, he calls such raw primordial experience an unnamed '*that*' which is not yet any definite '*what*'. '*It*' can only become a distinct thing when its implicit question '*what am I?*' begins to be answered by a '*which*'—something 'which' appears as 'this' or behaves as 'that', or has 'x' and 'y' and 'z' predicates. In the beginning *wasn't* the Word. It is humans who provide the words, the discrimination, and the grammar for the experience of reality; it is we who pick out and speak for its individual parts and their inter-relations. It is what we *have* to do in the overwhelming midst of things. To become human experience, the blur of pure sensational unnamed experience has to be filtered, adapted, and given a language, however partial, for survival's sake:

> the flux of it no sooner comes than it tends to fill itself with emphases, and these salient parts become identified and fixed and abstracted; so that experience now flows as if shot through with adjectives and nouns and prepositions and conjunctions.
>
> > (*Essays in Radical Empiricism*, chapter 3,
> > 'The Thing and its Relations')

Even when the basic language is there, it is those selected 'emphases' that register the tonal presence of an individual human creature, leaving its mark, taking it emotionally. As a '*fighter for ends*', for interests which but for the insistent pressure of human need, excitement, and emotion 'would have no status in the realm of being', James offers a voice for the race: 'Survival *shall* occur, and therefore organs *must* so work!' (*PP* 1, pp. 140–1, chapter 5, 'The Automaton Theory'). Even the most apparently impersonal and rationally argued philosophy, says James, is first marked and driven by the personal temperament of the philosopher, though conventionally this is hardly admitted. There is never the completely pure or the absolutely true.

Applied thought is shot through with individual need and interest, with personal intuition and emotional connection—with any nervous warmth that turns dead thoughts into hot and live ones. That is how this, and any, excited reader of William James becomes the application of his thinking, however rough and selective. Because James's unsystematized work, his work against systems, is resonantly incomplete: its involved reader becomes the attempted furthering of the thinking's completion, in another version of experimental practice. More than anything else—more than being a comprehensive systematizer, more than being a complete and autonomous artist—James finally found his purpose in wanting to be just that starting motor, that unashamedly useful catalyst, where intellectual moments involve psychological releases.

This will require in what follows some rough-and-ready handling, some pragmatic smash-and-grab of what matters in James's work. To achieve their fuller meaning and be useful, crucial moments and arresting sentences have to be taken out of their place and sequence, and put in a new context, in relation to their reader, for their use to be transmitted into other lives and other situations, for the thoughts to complete and fulfil themselves. In him they almost call out for that. But the very shape of some of these sentences is as vital as it is in more obviously literary works: they do need to be *read*, in a deep sense, in order deeply to work. 'Believe that life *is* worth living, and your belief will help create the fact' is not just what standard self-help books would airily translate into 'be positive'. The second clause ('will help create the fact') does not just come *after* the first ('Believe life is worth living'): it seems to come back round and lay the conditions for it. What could that mean, not just in syntax but in real life? is the question. Otherwise if it was just 'Have a positive outlook', why would it so excite me?

So I want to end with the first sentence that began my readerly experience of William James, before my knowing anything of the background story I've here outlined. It came in a casual skim through a chapter, 'What Pragmatism Means', printed as a single essay in an old second-hand Everyman's Library selection. It seems not so good now, just writing it out, because it was the act of coming upon it, by chance and in a certain rather stuck frame of mind, that gave it its moment, standing out from what had led up to it. 'The sequence is not simply first "*m*", then "*difference*", then "*n*"; but first "*m*", then "*difference*", then "*n-different-from-m*".' But even so, beside the underlying algebra, here is the experience of the *actual* words that I read, in their voice and flesh:

> Any idea upon which we can ride, so to speak; any idea that will carry us prosperously from any one part of our experience to any other part...

'Any that can, any that will' bears the tone that made me stop and start—and then after a few more words and emphases, the sentence completed itself:

> ...is true for just so much, true *instrumentally*.

'Any idea upon which we can ride, so to speak; any idea that will carry us prosperously from any one part of our experience to any other part is true, true instrumentally.'

I wanted its syntax to arrive at its completion, I wanted a whole sentence that made sense. It is 'about' thinking forward, thinking enabling some forward movement.[9] But then it was the *phrases* taken from there that remained, as though they were themselves insistently exhilarated things, electrical telegraphese to be spelt out again anew. It is '*Any* idea, any'; '*upon which* we can *ride*'; 'that will *carry* us'—and how those last two clauses, riding and carrying, were at once both slightly different and yet also equivalent in the mix of risk and trust. There were other words and phrases and thoughts scattered around the rest of the essays as I read on, that felt also excitingly semi-complete, awaiting further paraphrase and translation, their use or future not yet known. But still waiting: because the sheer surplus of surprise and excitement must have meant I was not sure I had really known this before, but had somehow needed it:—namely, that ideas were not static conclusions or final answers to arrive at, but *instruments* to *ride upon*, to give you forward movement. This felt different from what I had previously assumed. As if seeking permission, I had thought of any idea, Is this Right? Right as seen from outside or above; the impersonal and objective perspective as of something daunting and non-human there—or at least *imaginably* there—that all the time knew the permanent Truth. James may have thought of that Absolute as the false God, the cruel God—though for me the imagination of that haunting viewpoint of external judgment can never wholly go away. But here was something legitimately temporary: how thoughts that excite were like live and actual things that might *carry* us; ideas that could *help* me to *move towards* (…what, where?), or *get into fruitful relations with* (something…that he called *reality*). It was a code not fully worked out even in its urgent italics and emphases.

But leading into the next chapter, this energetic message, transmitted through verbs and gerunds, adverbs, prepositions, and conjunctions lifted out of completed sentences, gave thinking itself something to *go* on, something to go *with*. We talk all too ambitiously of Change but really what is vital, before or beneath that, is Movement: in place of stuckness, a 'consciousness of the *whence* and the *whither* which accompanies thinking in full flow' (*PP* 1, p. 242, chapter 9, 'The Stream of Thought').

2

THE PRAGMATIC GRAMMAR
OF WILLIAM JAMES

His friend, John Jay Chapman said that William James was not articulate in the exact way that a thinker should be. He had the gift of 'suggestion', rather than well-defined expression. His thought came out of his 'nature' rather than his 'intellect', and was never quite in sharp focus. It exhilarated but also exasperated Chapman that 'James was always throwing off sparks that were cognate only in this, that they came from the same central fire in him'.[1]

But that is just how I read his writings and ideas, as if they were expressions of a warm and fiery person. And I do so in the way that, as James himself says, a psychologist tries to get inside a complex person, to gain some sense of 'the sort of unuttered inner atmosphere in which his consciousness dwells alone with the secrets of its prison-house':

> This inner personal tone is what we can't communicate or describe articulately to others; but the wraith and ghost of it, so to speak, are often what our friends and intimates feel as our most characteristic quality.   ('The Gospel of Relaxation')

It is also, said James, what readers have to do: sense the personal flavour, the surrounding feel.

Though he knew the cost of his lack of formal clarity in terms of reception and reputation, James did not want to be the sort of philosopher Chapman desired. He wanted the central fire, the sparks. 'The definite images of psychology form but the very smallest part of our minds as they actually live. The traditional psychology talks like one who should say that a river consists of nothing but pailsful, spoonsful, quartpotsful, and other molded forms of water' (PP 1, p. 255, chapter 9, 'The Stream of Thought'). He valued instead the free-flowing water of consciousness, the actual living. The old classificatory psychology of the eighteenth century, listing separate faculties and different emotions, was both boring and unreal:

> the merely descriptive literature of the emotions is one of the most tedious parts of psychology. And not only is it tedious, but you feel that its subdivisions are to a great extent either fictitious or unimportant, and that its pretences to accuracy are a sham. But unfortunately there is little psychological writing about the emotions which is not merely descriptive.
>
> (PP 2, p. 448, chapter 25, 'The Emotions')

What James deplores is the mistake of wooden thinking that for each separate name there is automatically a distinct substance and entity. He did not deny fundamental emotions such as love and anger, joy or fear, or their roots in the basic survival reactions of attraction and aversion. But what went deepest for him was the *feeling* that went with any situation or experience, the surrounding felt sense of the thing that could not easily be defined. Nothing characterizes the ordinary academic and critical mind more, he lamented, than 'the extreme slowness' with which it faces 'wild facts, with no stall or pigeon-hole', or 'facts which threaten to break up the accepted system' ('What Psychical Research Has Accomplished').

The best psychological account of emotions in quick and living practice was provided instead by literature:

> As emotions are described in novels, they interest us, for we are made to share them. We have grown acquainted with the concrete objects and emergencies which calls them forth.
>
> (PP 2, p. 448, chapter 25, 'The Emotions')

What the literary way means here for James is human knowledge not as a 'knowing about' but an 'acquaintance with' or 'experience of'. It comes *before* we have got used to 'how to behave towards it, or how to meet the behaviour which we expect from it': 'Up to that point it is still "strange" to us' ('The Sentiment of Rationality'). Otherwise there is only the thinness of our traditional vocabulary for subjective experience, too slick in turning the strange and new into the all too recognizable and commonplace. In place of such ready-made, take-away information, it is literary thinking that makes the unfolding journey—the process of the reading and the writing—crucial to the very experience of meaning.

Here for example is a child who is usually active and interested, but then sometimes suffers fits of sudden depression:

> Then the mother would find the boy of three or four crying on the sofa.
>   'What's the matter?' she asked, and got no answer.
>   'What's the matter?' she insisted, getting cross.
>   'I don't know,' sobbed the child.

It is from chapter 3 of *Sons and Lovers* by D. H. Lawrence, in his youth a warm instinctive reader of James' *Principles of Psychology*, *Pragmatism*, and *The Varieties of Religious Experience*. But the strandedness of Paul Morel's 'I don't *know*' is not just about being a child, without sufficient words or experience. It is about something primordially deep which James understood in his sense of the vocabulary, grammar, and order of things: namely, that feelings come before we know them. It is not that we sob because we are unhappy, and the unhappiness logically causes the crying; but rather that we find we are unhappy because we are sobbing. The mind is not there to decide on having an emotion: it is in the body, deep in the pre-thinking of its nervous system, that the feeling first happens, unnamed. We *find* ourselves crying. It is that feeling of the sudden bodily change, mentally registered, that becomes the emotion.[2]

Even at a later stage of life, 'I don't know' remained crucial not because of inexperience but almost the opposite—because there was too much for immediate summary. In particular James found himself moved by the self-bafflement of Tolstoy and his character Levin in *Anna Karenina*. After the death of his brother, Levin is horrified at still having a life without the least knowledge of 'whence it came, what is it for, why, and what it is'. He cannot take that for granted, any more than James himself could, especially after the death of Minny Temple. Levin had tried to read the philosophers, but they only satisfied him whilst he was still reading them. Then when he came back to his life, he saw that he ought to be completely happy and yet—

> though he was a happy and healthy family man, Levin was several times so near to suicide that he hid a cord he had lest he should hang himself, and he feared to carry a gun lest he should shoot himself.
>
> But he did not hang or shoot himself and went on living.
>
> (*Anna Karenina*, Part 8, chapter 9)

'Though he was happy and healthy' is one thought; but 'so near to suicide…lest he should hang, lest he should shoot himself' looks like the major thought that still needs to be contained, however incongruously, in the same sentence. Yet the new paragraph 'But he did not…hang or shoot himself' is a third thought that silently takes the first ('happy and healthy') | into the second ('suicide') | and then beyond it—if only negatively ('did not') | to the end of the sentence ('and went on') | that is not a conclusion at all. What is more, that this 'But' was made a new paragraph is like a suddenly decisive alert, a change of pulse in the feeling. Some sort of micro-thinking is going on within and between these three movements, like a life twisting and turning upon itself to the bafflement of the man living it. 'Our heart-beats, our breathing, the pulses of our attention, fragments of words or sentences that pass through our imagination, people this dim habitat' (*PP* 1, p. 620, chapter 15, 'The Perception of Time'). And at the macro level of pained con-sciousness, of the honest but clumsy 'I', Levin is still perplexed by 'me': how could all this be, so discontinuously and contradictorily, together?

How *are* you? they might ask him, but people such as Levin are too earnest to know how to reply truthfully. Yet with William James, it should almost be 'how am *me*?' The I–Me distinction he invented[3] makes Me the person, the empirical core; whereas I is the thinker, sometimes venturing forth into the world, trying it out ahead, but always consciously reporting on the effects on Me, behind it. That anterior Me is not inert or invulnerable but like a heart always capable of being affected and changed, and is never simply covered or wholly known by its I, however much I can detect its relative movements from good to bad, from worse to better.

All this made for an idea that, via James, I could 'go with' at the different level of thinking that literature allowed, in order to find a deeper 'me' or 'it'. It was a seemingly technical idea which really, like writing itself, only used the technical at the micro-level to avoid the tameness of superficial paraphrase. The idea was to do with syntax and sequence, and trying to *point* to moments within them. Amidst the run of vital micro-movements, that might also mean trying to count the number of separate thoughts, pointed out, in any chosen sentence or sequence of sentences, even as they turn in different or changing directions. That is what I was doing in counting—1, 2, 3—the different movements in those few words from *Anna Karenina* as Levin himself wonders what could possibly be holding them together. Then, acting not by abstract definition but in actual practice:

(i)   you will see for a moment what you think a separate thought *is*; and then

(ii) see again that the separate thoughts are not so really separate, after all, and

(iii) there is not just, say, two thoughts, but a third thing that has to hold the two together in a syntax, a thinker, and a person.

That's the shift from static to dynamic which a creative sentence truly makes. 'Let anyone try to cut a thought across in the middle and get a look at its section, and he will see how difficult the introspective observation of the transitive tracts is' (*PP* 1, p. 244, chapter 9, 'The Stream of Thought'): one part shades into another.

What is vital here is subtle transition, and trying to read between the lines, in the very interstices of things:

Life is in the transitions as much as in the terms connected; often, indeed it seems to be there more emphatically, as if our spurts and sallies forward were the real line of battle...In this line we live prospectively as well as retrospectively. It is 'of' the past, inasmuch as it comes expressly as the past's continuation; it is 'of' the future in so far as the future, when it comes, will have continued it.

('A World of Pure Experience')

'*Life* is in the transitions...' This is emphatically not the 'knowing about' that is post-mortem naming. By that act of naming, 'the continuous flow of the mental stream is sacrificed, and in its place, an atomism, a brickbat plan of construction, is preached' (*PP* 1, pp. 196, chapter 7, 'The Methods and Snares of Psychology'). It is like saying 'that cyanide of potassium kills because it is a "poison", or that it is cold tonight because it is "winter", or that we have five fingers because we are "pentadactyls"':

These are but names for the facts, taken from the facts, and then treated as previous and explanatory.

(*Pragmatism*, lecture 7, 'Pragmatism and Humanism')

We offer these so-called 'explanations', says James, but actually, in reality, there is nothing 'behind' the facts; there is just the sheerness of their existence. In James' grammar, facts are not first construed as 'true'—it is odder than that, it is prior to that: in themselves facts 'simply *are*', full-stop (*Pragmatism*, lecture 6, 'Pragmatism's Conception of Truth'). They are the 'given' in the world from which any thinking has then to proceed. 'Reality, life, experience, concreteness, immediacy, use what word you will, exceeds our logic, overflows and surrounds it' (a *Pluralistic Universe*, chapter 5, 'The Compounding of Consciousness').

In fact, James is marvellous at imaginatively recalling how a now-fossilized idea first came dynamically into life, and why it once felt so good. He can imagine what it must have felt like for our lowest ancestors to move in a dangerous world that at every moment seemed unique, unrecognizable, and wholly contingent. And then for such vulnerable creatures, with just sufficient consciousness to feel helpless without understanding: imagine, again, how wonderful to be able to move into a second world that through their developing resources of memory and reason became more safe and predictable, on the basis of knowing what had gone before. Then the first basic feeling of discovery was *'the same again'* (*Pragmatism*, lecture 5 'Pragmatism and Common Sense'): we had this before, and likely it will return in future too. 'This *sense of sameness* is the very keel and backbone of our thinking' (*PP* 1, p. 459, chapter 12, 'Conception'). We no longer have to be creatures always overwhelmed by an emotion or an event that seems to have no cause or precedent behind it.

But what was at first so amazingly useful settles into becoming habitual and teachable, down the generations. It is the economy of evolution's next stage, conserving energy, consolidating knowledge by turning past discoveries into present commonplaces. And then the habitual tends to harden into the over-secure, over-mechanical, and over-systematic, turning into a substitute world. It is at this stage that there is to James's mind the revisionary need 'to break the rules that have become too narrow for the actual case' ('The Moral Philosopher and the Moral Life'), to seek renewal, to recognize the untamed and the anomalous, and to make discoveries again. We have five fingers because we are 'pentadactyls'! No more of such verbal tautology, such vicious intellectualism, says James.

James's grammar is more about act than talk. For him it is pointing rather than naming that is the first crucial act of human attention. 'I must *point*, point to the mere *that* of life, and you by inner sympathy must fill out the *what* for yourselves' (*A Pluralistic Universe*, lecture 7, 'The Continuity of Experience'). And 'the minimum'—the germ and starting point of cognition—'must be named by the word that says the least…as *lo! there! eco! voilà!*' (*PP* 1, p. 222, chapter 8, 'The Relations of Mind to Other Things'). William James is the great sentence-writer in italics, the great maker of emphases, the great user of deictic monosyllables so basic that you would hardly think to look them up in a dictionary. The, It, That, What, There, Here, This: 'Subjective interest may, by laying its weighty index-finger on particular items of experience, so accent them as to give to the least frequent associations far more power to shape our thought than the most frequent ones possess' (*PP* 1, p. 403, chapter 11, 'Attention').

Pointing is where language begins, when someone first physically and then audibly points to an object of actual perception in the outside world. And from that use of a basic language working directly within the world, there develops through human evolution a shift of register, such that the language becomes also a medium in itself, a symbolic representation of that world on a mapped and written page. There, to sustain the task of pointing at a new and higher level of orientation and meaning, human language begins to develop its own internal resources: a language-within-language that now points out its own interconnections, parentheses, and meta-commentaries; looks forward or turns back on itself, becomes questioning and reflective upon itself. And yet it is a language that must not get securely sealed off: it has always to be wary of its own tendency to become a name-like substitute or a closed system. So that, with exploration instead of explanation, the thoughts it allows contain an unknown and changing mix of self and world.

And this is what I am saying, with James, is still needed, as the first dumb instrument or tool in the psychology of reading and writing and thinking. That we should simply point to '*what*' matters or '*where*' it matters; then, says James, the '*that*' to which you point is implicitly 'a thing that asks "*What* am I?"' (*A Pluralistic Universe*, lecture 5, 'The Compounding of Consciousness'). Thinking is not first of all about articulacy, it is about being able to point the index-finger at the powerful place, the hot spot, from which everything else follows. This is what I will call James' agnosticism, the most powerful investigative form of 'What am I?...I don't know'. It is from not-yet-knowing that its quest starts and often has to re-start—without ready-made verbal pigeonholes for what James called the 'unclassified' matter of experience.[4]

This chapter is about learning this vital thinking-language from William James. It works via the blind feeling of some tendency that we go along with, trying to sense 'from where' and 'to where' it is going, in some mental equivalent of prepositions. In this way, James put what he called an inchoate 'vagueness' back into the world, for all Chapman's dismay: 'It is the reinstatement of the vague to its proper place in our mental life that I am so anxious to press on the attention' (*PP* 1, p. 254, chapter 9, 'The Stream of Thought'). It is less like a slow word-by-word language than a sort of fluid inner music, shaping itself through its rhythmic pulse, one set of sounds altering the next it feeds into, prior to any sharply-bounded naming. To James, the sentences feel their way: the clauses are 'cognitive of one another', are relations 'immediately conscious of continuing each other', even by means of 'but' as much as 'and' ('A World of Pure Experience').

It is this half-blind sensing process that, through reading William James, the twentieth-century Austrian musicologist Victor

Zuckerkandl recognized as the language of music itself, without concepts. Imagine, he says, the situation of a one-dimensional creature whose living space is the line along which it moves. It wants to know more about its condition and purpose, but it cannot step out of the line, to look at it from outside. What it can only do is use its senses to move forwards. Yet though it may only move along the line, within that it can make experience more than merely linear.[5] As it feels its way, the creature tries by a kind of blind musical or poetical intelligence to bring what was backward into relation to what it intuits ahead, to feel its own movements up and down, back and forth, and forge some harmony.

This kind of thinking is not under the control of a determining I, as thinker. James says that it is more like an *It* that thinks through the process: 'If we could say in English "it thinks", as we say "it rains" or "it blows" '—without having to know quite what 'it' fully refers back to—then 'we should be stating the fact most simply and with the minimum of assumption' (*PP* 1, pp. 224–5, chapter 9, 'The Stream of Thought'). I love that 'minimum of assumption': I want the speed and pressure of the thinking to preclude as far as possible the slow lumbering work of tame presupposition or explanation, and just go on instead with what it finds, not stopping to try to know exactly what guarantees it. It's not ideal in any sense, it's pragmatic, it is where we are, and it takes its chances.

The Tool-kit

There is a vital difference in the meaning of the same word when it is taken 'statically' as a separate name, and when it is used 'dynamically in a sentence' within a human context (PP 1, p. 265, chapter 9, 'The Stream of Thought').

Take for example a crucial word in James' thinking: '*chance*'. It is a word that tries to place the anomalous or the unexpected, to categorize all that otherwise cannot be so.

To the ancient Greek philosophers, it was the lower world that was defined by 'mere' chance. Chance meant that muddle of apparently contingent happenings and reasonless accidents in the midst of life which insulted intelligence and offended its love of harmony, by seeming to offer no higher law, no permanent category, or single clarifying cause.[6] But in his essay 'The Dilemma of Determinism', James insists that he wants to keep the word and put it to use, for why should it be so offensive? The sting in the word 'chance', he says, lies in thinking it means something definite, a positive Thing that makes only for whatever is irrational. He turns on the word 'positive':

> Now chance means nothing of the kind. It is a purely negative and relative term, giving us no information about that of which it is predicated, except that it happens to be disconnected with something else — not controlled, secured, or necessitated by other things in advance of its own actual presence.

Suddenly there is some sense that 'negative' is not what we usually take it to imply. 'Chance' as a noun is not a definite thing, but only a blanket term for what is indefinite, for happenings not covered by our system of predicting. 'Purely negative' here means: 'It escapes, and says Hands off!, coming when it comes, as a free gift, or not at all' ('The Dilemma of Determinism') It is just what happens—*not* immediately known, *in*determinate, *im*precise and *un*classified. There is *no* guarantee whether the chance-thing turns out good or bad, but whatever it is, it is for its moment its own thing, apparently unconditioned by what was before it and what is around it, an unexplained particular that does not at once fit into a predictable system. Hence the negative only means it is something given or presented, and as such it becomes less a noun than a verb, offering the fighting chance and risk of freedom. The so-called 'negativeness'—which he wonderfully re-names 'this opacity of the chance-thing'—

> does not preclude its having any amount of positiveness and luminosity from within, and at its own place and moment. All that its chance-character asserts about it is that there is something in it really of its own, something that is not the unconditional property of the whole. If the whole wants this property, it must wait to get it... ('The Dilemma of Determinism')

James thought it was a pity that English was not an inflected language like Greek and Latin in which the same word could have different endings depending on its grammatical function in any sentence: verbs that can be conjugated, nouns and their adjectives that can be declined as subject and object, and so on. Nature working within those contextually adaptive word-forms 'did not appear inalterable, but changed their shape to suit the context in which they lay. It must have been easier then than now to conceive of the same object as being thought of at different times in non-identical conscious states' (PP 1, pp. 236–7, chapter 9, 'The Stream of Thought'). But in a way, it is a more reanimating surprise when James, like a poet, can make a word such as 'chance' alter in front of our eyes without any forewarning sign, only 'the jolt, jolt, jolt' half-hidden within the onward course of linear reading.[7] James make the reader feel that a key word has a wilder emphasis of its own, untamed in the midst of a sentence. It bursts out through the power of spontaneous selection triggered by the needs and pressures of the meaning. That word 'opacity' rather than the more usual 'mystery', for example: 'mystery' would feel less unique and more consciously value-laden, whereas 'opacity', to use James' own words, 'instantaneously fills a socket completely moulded to its shape' (*PP* 1, p. 588, chapter 14, 'Association'). It feels right, it does credit to the unknown surprise. Suddenly, the sheer re-description of the word—the shift of life from static to dynamic, from atom to action, and from opacity from without, to 'luminos-ity from within'—makes it what Keats said of any real idea: the new centre of a possible intellectual world,[8] changing if only ever so slightly the unthought assumptions of the old conventional world view. Experience 'has ways of *boiling over*, and making us correct our present formulas' (*Pragmatism*, lecture 6, 'Pragmatism's Conception of Truth'). This is why Whitehead believed that with such overflow of thinking in James, 'philosophy is akin to poetry'.[9] Then the ways thoughts happen or words come is like poetry; or rather, poetry is like this, when life is creative. It is never complete, there is never a final word:

> After all that reason can do has been done, there still remains the opacity of the finite facts as merely given, with most of their pecu-liarities mutually unmediated and unexplained....
> ('Preface' to The Will to Believe and Other Essays')

The 'negative', the 'alogical', the sheer 'opacity' and 'givenness' of things, James goes on, can never be wholly eradicated, and he adds, should not be: 'Not unfortunately the universe is wild'—whatever we would like to think, or not think, about it. *Not unfortunately* is a formulation that fights against conservatism; but equally, it registers that nothing is truly wild if it is too easily called fortunate. 'The idea of chance is, at bottom, exactly the same thing as the idea of *gift*—the one simply being a disparaging, the other a eulogistic name for anything on which we have no effective claim' ('The Dilemma of Determinism'). Again, the feeling of 'no effective claim' goes deeper into the nature of life than the specific emotions we may or must have about that.

But it is not just language as vocabulary. Near the very beginning of *Science and the Modern World* (1926), Whitehead singled out what William James, finishing the *Principles of Psychology*, wrote to his brother Henry: 'I have to forge every sentence in the teeth of irreducible and stubborn facts.' That was the two-way force of an achieved sentence: to feel in it a resistance from the world that nonetheless stimulates the human effort to take it on. What I found and still find astonishing is the way-round of grammar in James's struggle. It is not just that 'we' do the thinking, or that 'I' do the struggling to recall, and there is always first-person control. That is the sort of institutionalization of thought, built into the very structure of our language, subject–verb–object, that James always wants to break out of—only, not by creating a wholly new syntax but by making the need for one erupt within the pressure on the old. This is the subtle micro-work James loves instead:

> There is not a conjunction or a preposition, and hardly an adverbial phrase, syntactic form, or inflection of voice, in human speech, that does not express some shading or other of relation which we at some moment actually feel to exist between the larger objects of our insight....
>
> We ought to say a feeling of *and*, a feeling of *if*, a feeling of *but*, and a feeling of *by*, quite as readily as we say a feeling of *blue* or a feeling of *cold*. Yet we do not: so inveterate has our habit becoming of recognizing the existence of the substantive parts alone...
>
> (*PP* 1, pp. 245–6, chapter 9, 'The Stream of Thought')

'Shadings': these are the subtle feelings—of 'it' or 'but' or 'with'—that go deeper than single named emotions. These instrumental conjunctions and prepositions are some of the least noticed signs of our organism's feeling for life; and we can't fully know the reality that lies deeper in these interstices than in most of our concepts. But we can use their grammar as the life of thinking in action. 'We can not, it is true, *name* our different living "ands" or "withs" except by naming the different terms towards which they are moving us, but we *live* their specifications and differences before those terms explicitly arrive' ('Is Radical Empiricism Solipsistic?'). I am astonished all over again to think that we can live some things, and use them and even point to them, better than we can ever know them.

Conventional thinking is too chunky to do its work in living time. That which Philosophy denotes by the name 'the Present' is what James calls a specious present, 'really part of the past—a recent past—delusively given as being a time that intervenes between the past and the future'. Whereas in experience there is not those three separate blocks of time:

> Its *content* is in a constant flux, events dawning into its forward end as fast as they fade out of its rearward one, and each of them changing its time-coefficient from 'not yet', or 'not quite yet', to 'just gone' or 'gone' as it passes by.
>
> (PP 1, pp. 609, 630, chapter 15, 'The Perception of Time')

Hence the nerve-like blind indicators in the search for meaning: 'of', 'not yet' and 'just gone'; 'with', 'near', 'from', 'towards'; 'and', 'if', 'but'—all of them 'expectant of a "more" to come' ('Is Radical Empiricism Solipsistic?'). It is by its movements in time, through secret inner transitions, relations, and psychological interstices, that we best work out what and where we are, as we go along.

Philosophy has always turned on grammatical particles. With, near, next, like, from, towards, against, because, for, through, my — these words designate types of conjunctive relation arranged in a roughly ascending order of intimacy and inclusiveness....We can imagine a universe of withness but no nextness; or one of nextness but no likeness, or of likeness with no activity, or of activity with no purpose, or of purpose with no ego. These would be universes, each with its own grade of unity. The universe of human experience is, by one or another of its parts, of each and all those grades.

('A World of Pure Experience')

So many possible worlds and dimensions and combinations are enfolded within this world. For a moment in time otherwise so small that we can barely register it, those little unfolding words – 'withness', 'nextness'—hold on to the specious present, as well-nigh non-existent or impenetrable as it is. For between the environment's outward stimulus and the creature's physical response, mind is itself the equivalent of a transitive state, an attempted modifying conjunction, both an 'and' and a 'but'.

And James reveals this mentality in his own writing, even as he here explains the process of the transitive parts. I now put in the italics myself, as pointers, amidst what passes so swiftly:

Now it is very difficult, introspectively, to see the transitive parts for what they really are. If they are *but* flights to a conclusion, *stopping* them to look at them *before* the conclusion is reached, is *really annihilating* them. *Whilst if* you wait till the conclusion *be* reached, it *so* exceeds them in vigour and stability that it *quite* eclipses and swallows *them up in* its glare.

(*PP* 1, pp. 243–4, chapter 9, 'The Stream of Thought')

This is the feel of syntax, live, in the shaping of mind: it is a barely noticeable enabler, swallowed up in its own enabling. It also marks why human voices are not monotones, are sub-consciously always selecting emphasis and accents through a kind of background music. A particular word matters—hence the temporary hold of the changed tone or the delaying conjunction or the subordinate clause—before it must also yield itself to being part of a sentence which now overtakes it in completion of itself. That means that the most creative life often lies in the little in-between places devoid of conscious articulate content, the gaps, the would-be means and niches, forgotten as soon as filled, made or used, because the effort is always to what they might lead.

In a recent interview a writer of both fiction and non-fiction said that when she wrote non-fiction she really had to make up her mind about her line of argument and then follow a clear direction. But the great freedom of fiction was that she could admit the complexity, feel the emotional textures, and search out the feeling of it happening, rather than the line you should take.[10] But as what I am calling a literary thinker William James tried to obey no such clear distinction. For him the greatest achievement of a sentence in any form or genre is when, for all its linear appearance, it is no longer a straight line of sameness or causation, the line of least resistance. The object of attention has so many aspects that we are often rightly deflected from our original direction and find our thinking suddenly following something different from what we started with, 'we know not why'. But it means the burgeoning of new sentences, of different conjunctions and relations: 'Our earlier lines, having grown irrelevant, are then dropped...because of so many new dimensions into which experience has opened. Instead of a straight line, it now follows a zig-zag' (A Pluralistic Universe, Appendix C, 'On the Notion of Reality as Changing'). The lines are only partial members of a different and larger potential shape, 'a vast natural network' with even 'the smallest real datum being both a coming and a going', allowing infinitesimal tendencies to diversification.

> Things are 'with' one another in many ways, but nothing includes everything, or dominates over everything. The word 'and' trails along after every sentence. Something always escapes. 'Ever not quite' has to be said of the best attempts made anywhere... The word 'or' names a genuine reality.
>
> (A Pluralistic Universe, 'Conclusions')

The reality is not a straightforward matter of 'all' or 'none'. My philosophy stands out, says James,

> for the legitimacy of the notion of *some*: each part of the world is in some ways connected, in some other ways not connected with its other parts. (*A Pluralistic Universe*, lecture 2, 'Monistic Idealism')

In the complex syntax, 'the connecting *is* the thinking' (*Talks to Teachers*, 'Memory').

What does this mean in practice? I think Robert Frost knew what it meant when he wrote in his essay 'The Figure a Poem Makes', 'The impressions most useful to my purpose seem always those I was unaware of and so made no note of at the time':

> like giants we are always hurling experience ahead of us to pave the future with against the day when we may want to strike a line of purpose across it for somewhere. The line will have the more charm for not being mechanically straight. We enjoy the straight crookedness of a good walking stick.

This, says Frost, is 'a better wildness', the logic of the line followed forward is revealed only backwards, in retrospect.

It was from this tool-kit of pointers and seekers, leads, instruments and verb-like words and prompts, that I have learnt a language and a grammar, or rather, realized they were already intuitively latent in the lines and brain waves of thought. For these particles are themselves proto-thoughts, the very instruments of language and thinking 'in the making'[11] to use James' signature phrase, *and* a tiny subtly enabling means by which to track the mind's evanescent inner processes. Otherwise we can hardly catch them or make them out:

> The rush of the thought is so headlong that it almost always brings us up at the conclusion before we can arrest it....As a snowflake crystal caught in the warm hand is no longer a crystal but a drop, so, instead of catching the feeling of relation moving to its term, we find we have caught some substantive thing, usually the last word we were pronouncing, statically taken...The attempt at introspective analysis [is like] trying to turn up the gas quickly enough to see how the darkness looks.
>
> (PP 1, p. 244, chapter 9, 'The Stream of Thought')

But literary thinking, in fiction or non-fiction, overflowing the limits of description and explanation, at least lets its reader *see* those electric traces even as they are left behind through their very use. A mind is working on this page, the conjunctions and prepositions are thinking for and with and from their writer. This in turn is one of the best reasons for the existence of literary criticism, reading in practice, reading with attention: to be able to see again, and to retrace more slowly, another's words working as a means of seeking—without losing the sense of how fast and how warm the process remains. 'Heaving into uncreated space' is how Lawrence describes it in his Study of Thomas Hardy' (chapter 5), with all the power of that '*un*created' about to be created. The writers make their turns and emphases, and the readers can follow the same pathway of mental orientation, mentally pointing or marking in the margin this and that indicator, and not letting it all go past. Otherwise 'the mass of our thinking vanishes for ever, beyond hope of recovery', and even psychology 'only gathers up a few of the crumbs that fall from the feast' (*PP* 1, p. 276, chapter 9, 'The Stream of Thought').

This is how a sentence is for James a model of living in time, revealing what is so infinitely continuous, subtle, and shaded. In the sensational stream of actual experience:

> The concrete pulses of experience appear pent in by no such definite limits as our conceptual substitutes for them are confined by. They run into each other and seem to interpenetrate...There is no datum so small as not to show this mystery, if mystery it be. The tiniest feeling that we can possibly have comes with an earlier and a later part and with a sense of their continuous precession.
>
> (*A Pluralistic Universe*, lecture 7, 'The Continuity of Experience')

That is the medium within which we swim, with that extraordinary mixture of permeable boundaries and minutely affective places en route—the very passage of what we have to think of as one thing moving into another though there is nothing literally in between to separate them. It is almost impossible to take in. You can never quite catch your own process. But the literary-type sentence can do so, as the hybrid between writing and living, between experiencing and thinking: it can combine clauses with flow, allow conceptual moments a temporary fix within a nonetheless ongoing mergence. It models James' horizontal efforts, the attempt to find a way forward.

This is also how grammar, made into syntax, is for James a model for a deeper psychology. For example, he takes the word 'is' and the words 'let it be'. When an idea *stings* us in one way, says James, making us feel an electric connection with it, we believe it

is a reality; when it stings us in another way and makes what feels
to be a different connection with our self, we say, *let it be* a reality.
To each grammatical mood there corresponds a different attitude
of consciousness: 'The indicative and the imperative moods are as
much ultimate categories of thinking as they are of grammar...It
is a relation to our life. It means *our* adoption of the things, *our* caring for them, *our* standing by them...' (PP 2, pp. 568–9, chapter 26,
'Will'). The shift from 'don't care', or 'merely considering an object
as possible', to 'deciding or willing it to be real': that is 'the change
from the fluctuating to the stable personal attitude concerning it'
(PP 2, p. 569). To make the possible into the real; the bare things
into our caring for them: that is the human difference.

So James is moved by Walt Whitman's lines to his reader, 'whoever you are', 'that you be my poem':

None have understood you, but I understand you;
None have done justice to you — you have not done justice to yourself

'You have not known what you are'; James loves how the great
bursting voice of the poet and the poem now remedies those
omissions, in a present tense for ever emotionally rescuing what
has been suppressed and unheard in the real (*Pragmatism*, lecture 7,
'Pragmatism and Religion'). When the link there should be
between a person's inner truth and its recognition in the world is
absent—'None have understood you'—that is the moral tragedy
of human life. Then some potentially enlarging idea or ideal in a
person 'never wholly resolves, never gets its voice out of the minor
into the major key, or its speech out of the subjunctive into the
imperative mood' (PP 2, p. 547, chapter 26, 'Will'). Only something
like an act within syntax could get what was half-hidden in a

subordinate clause, a minor key, out into a main and major one, as Zuckerkandl would have it. Or as Whitman boldly puts it, across all measures and directions of time, 'I should have made my way to you long ago'—in a way that makes your mind spin. But otherwise so much fails, has been wasted, or lost, as James knew his own father's work had mainly been. 'None have done justice to you—you have not done justice to yourself.' Rescue the minor key; in any settlement of meaning or dispute, still include at least traces of what has had to be excluded.

All these things are an implicit guide to a way of life: horizontal, forward, looking for something to go on from, to go on to; knowing that much that is in excess or inchoate and vague will not get realized, but trying to shift what can be from the minor to the major key. I don't want words of explicit, normalized encouragement; I don't want to write a book entitled 'how William James can save your life'. I want signs, instruments, and directions towards knowing how to be able to *do* something, to *get* somewhere, to *realize* more. And in that effort if we know more of what goes on in the transitional spaces, we may be able to believe in and employ them more, to create subtler and deeper effects.

The Meaning of 'O'

Chapman complained that for all his remarkable articulacy James was actually at some deep level inarticulate. James himself wanted blind pointing to have the priority over verbal facility. He was interested in what he could 'not-ever-quite' think about or easily put into words, that vague, latent or implicit feel which was like the surrounding resonance of memory. It meant, as we say, biting off more than he could chew. And only if he got himself into the right place, a full place, could he do real thinking. The right place being, that is to say, some sense of an area in life that felt emotionally vital, that felt full of uncategorized matter that one wanted and needed to know more of and go forward from. That is what pointing is to do with: locating a key place and trying to be within it even when it feels problematic. Hence this brilliant analogy for the strongly felt pre-verbal sense that is prior to explicit thinking, and that explicit thinking comes out of:

> Suppose we try to recall a forgotten name. The state of our consciousness is peculiar. There is a gap therein; but no mere gap. It is a gap that is intensely active. A sort of wraith of the name is in it, beckoning us in a given direction...If wrong names are proposed to us, this singularly definite gap acts immediately so as to negate them. They do not fit the mould. And the gap of one word does not feel like the gap of another, all empty of content as both might seem... (PP 1, p. 251, chapter 9, 'The Stream of Thought')

'What's the word? I can't get it, can't remember it': there for once the mind's background process, usually hidden by what it is working on, is experienced in itself. This charged blankness, this tip-of-the-tongue feeling is like looking for the 'right' word in a way that at its most serious a poet does. That is how words best 'come' in James, as upsurges fitting the inner shape of the gap as if it were a mould. It is related to what in 'The Constant Symbol' made Robert Frost call a poem 'the emotion of having a thought'. But it is also, more generally, like the experience of finding a problem: the yearning sense of something that is needed to fill a gap and fall into place, as solution. 'To hit upon a problem,' wrote the philosopher Michael Polanyi in sentences that help in just the way that

James helps, 'is the first step to any discovery and indeed to any creative act. To see a problem is to see something hidden that may yet be accessible.'[12] The problem is not so much an obstacle as that which first creates the right place for excited thought to start from, for the hidden that may yet be accessible. Another of James's readers, Bruce Mangan speaks of how problem-solving is the process of establishing a surrounding field or environment 'which can later recognise a solution when it occurs'; where perhaps 'the very process of creating such a problem-solving context itself moves us toward a solution'. On this view, he concludes, 'aesthetic experience is an artifact of the problem-solving function of consciousness', and from an evolutionary perspective, 'it appears to be the accidental outcome of a cognitive process developed for purely pragmatic, biological ends'.[13] In its adaptive uses, the brain does not know or care whether it is being asked to remember a word, to solve a problem, or to make a sentence better—it is all about the 'active' gap and looking for what will fit its mould:

> a gap we cannot yet fill with a definite picture, word, or phrase, but which, in the manner described…influences us in an intensely active and determinate psychic way…. To fill it up is our thought's destiny.   (PP 1, p. 259, chapter 9, 'The Stream of Thought')

If one error was to suppose that every word stood 1:1 for some separate thing in the world, then the opposite mistake was to suppose that the *lack* of a word meant no entity could be there. 'It is hard to focus our attention on the nameless' (PP 1, p. 195, chapter 6, 'The Methods and Snares of Psychology'). But the nameless gap was what James most looked for in thought. Through selection by pragmatic trial and error, some images or phrases seem to have greater relation than others to this aching gap: we can at least tell if they are getting us nearer or further. That is why it is so important not prematurely to fill the hole with 'escape-route' substitutes or 'that'll do' paraphrases, until it is too late to go back, revise, and find what was first felt as potently missing. Nouns are too often literal *stop-gaps* (*A Pluralistic Universe*, chapter 5, 'The Compounding of Consciousness'). True articulacy, says James, should be more like the children's blindfold game in search of some object, guided by the directive 'warmer' or 'colder' en route. Then suddenly, with what feels like the right word, 'there is something that gives a click inside of us, a bell that strikes' ('The Will to Believe'). If the words 'come',

> it will seem as if the striving itself had drawn or pulled them into actuality out from the state of merely possible being in which they were. How is this feat performed? How does the pulling *pull*? How do I get my hold on words not yet existent, and when they come by what means have I *made* them come? Really it is the problem of creation; for in the end the question is: How do I make them *be*? Real activities are those which really make things be, without which the things are not, and with which they are there.
>
> (*A Pluralistic Universe*, Appendix B, 'The Experience of Activity')

That is how James is a psychologist of mental life rather than mental illness. Whatever struggles to be creative has its reward not *after* its efforts, as in the award of a degree or a diploma, but simultaneously in the very exercise of them as a greater vitality. So it is the gap that is active, it is the thought that is the thinker and that has a 'destiny'. And there seems to me no point in saying that it is still really 'us', not 'it', because that's not how it is felt and experienced; and more, that is not how it has to be felt in order to work. Something in the mind that might eventually become substantiated into an 'I' feels there is a word for this, there is a future solution somewhere ahead; another part acting as the active gap, a background sense of potential rightness, keeps calling for an answer to meet it. All we have to do is set up that tension and wait intently till something comes as of itself out of that force-field. There is no time or place to introduce an 'I' there, the 'I' hardly yet knows what to think. That is what A. N. Whitehead thought was James's most revolutionary contribution, in the sentence: 'The passing Thought then seems to be the Thinker'; it does not need some extra substance to think it twice-over. 'The thought simply *comes*' (*PP* I, pp. 342, 345, chapter 10, 'The Consciousness of Self').

What I am saying here arises out of that idea of the children's blindfold game, and, again, that sentence of James's about their being in the mind hot spots, places created by live ideas, feelings, and beliefs, as opposed to cold and dead ones. It means that as versions of feeling one's way, the 'pragmatic' in exploratory thinking, the 'aesthetic' in writing and reading, and the 'agnostic' within religion are all versions of the same mental thing: the almost over-full place in which all the not-knowing has to go, the place of instability between extreme chaos and complete order, across the range of difference and sameness.

Warmer or colder, says the childhood game. But in the adult world, psychology after James offers a different agnostic or aesthetic instrument for orientation ahead of knowing or naming that I also want to bring into harness. It is what the psychoanalyst W. R. Bion took from the philosopher A. N. Whitehead, the mathematical term 'o', used by Bion to signify 'O' for origin as well as 'o' for zero.

It is a pointer towards what Bion calls the 'really real': an unnameable but regulative sense of reality, an 'It', obscured within the phenomenal world of human beings but felt amongst it, even so, as the force of a never quite attainable truth. 'o' was a tool or steer within deep analysis, in the dark of the psyche, to indicate a patient's proximity to or distance from that place which most mattered in their case. When vocabulary can be overcharged with inherited and premature implications, Bion wanted to try to use algebraic or geometric notations, letters, indicators, instead of precipitate nouns and unrespectful categories; seeking to give a blind pointer to intensity, without too soon imposing an interpretation. For Bion, as for James, thought was not the product of thinking but the other way round. Thoughts sought a thinker, became their own thinker. Our conventional line, as to which did what, produced fundamental misunderstandings:

> Reality is not something which lends itself to being known. It is impossible to know reality for the same reason that makes it impossible to sing potatoes; they may be grown, or pulled, or eaten, but not sung. Reality has to be 'been': there should be a transitive verb 'to be' expressly for use with the term 'reality'.
>
> (*Transformations*, London: Heinemann, 1965, p. 148)

Again, in situations beyond the norms and outside what is traditional, our grammar and vocabulary can hardly cope without bland distortion.

But for James himself, the formulation '*as if*' serves as one of his greatest pragmatic particles, as a launch pad for speculative thinking or a go-ahead for imaginative intuition. It is as if, says James, we are iron bars blindly placed within a magnetic field, with the feeling of *something there*, the agnostic sense of a reality that goes deeper than the ordinary senses of sight and touch and hearing:

> It is as if a bar of iron, without touch or sight, with no representative faculty whatever, might nevertheless be strongly endowed with

an inner capacity for magnetic feeling; and as if, through the various arousals of its magnetism by magnets coming and going in its neighbourhood, it might be consciously determined to different attitudes and tendencies. Such a bar of iron could never give you an outward description of the agencies that had the power of stirring it so strongly; yet of their presence, and their significance for its life, it would be intensely aware through every fibre of its being.

(VRE, p. 50, lecture 3, 'The Reality of the Unseen')

Of course, James does not think humans are simply iron bars, mechanically determined by magnets. But when something we encounter—someone we meet, or something we read or think—has a force to move and activate us, then we have an extra sense of 'what' and 'where' life is for us, like a message to us living in the middle of things without clear principles and goals. He loves it that there may be something dumb in us that cannot fully represent what nonetheless we are intensely aware of as stirring every fibre of our being: it is called 'that', it could as well be 'o'. It points, it seeks, it monitors a sense of unexpected rightness or sudden fit. It is what James feels when he reads religious writings without feeling himself as religious as their writers—they are testimonies 'to which something in me makes admiring response': 'no doubt there is a germ in me of something similar that makes response'.[14] It is, as so often in James' vocabulary and grammar, not an 'I' but that vaguely-definite 'something' 'in me' that is drawn to respond. And it responds because it feels it corresponds: 'ideas are so much flat psychological surfaces unless some mirrored matter gives them a cognitive lustre' (The Meaning of Truth, chapter 8, 'The Pragmatist Account of Truth'). Something in me feels a relation to something equivalently out there, like its other half. And to James relations are as much, and probably more, reality as any of the separate things that are related.

I often feel like James' bar of iron, excitedly innocent or unsure of what exactly it is I am attracted to and why so. These are inklings albeit with strong feelings, something small to start from, yet latent with something bigger than itself. For James, it is not the big generalizations, grand statements, or lumpen solutions that he believes in; it is more 'the invisible molecular moral forces' that work their way through 'the crannies of the world' in order to create concrete movements, individual achievements that even so are seldom recognized immediately in the world.[15] It is in the 'crepuscular depths of personality' that 'the sources of all our outer deeds and decisions take their rise' ('Is Life Worth Living?'). The tiny enabling grammatical particles pointing to 'o' are like those molecular forces, their micro-potential materializing the movements of those depths of personality in trying to find a way. It is the creative 'how' of our arriving at some specific end-point that James cares about, making the 'what' all that it finally is: otherwise it is just an abstraction not the upshot of a process. But equally the 'how' only has its purpose in the 'what' it looks to arrive at on any particular occasion, in the potential made real as at the end of a great sentence-like effort.

That's why William James wryly contrasted his syntax with that of his brother, Henry, comparing the novelist's circumlocutory manner with what he called his own cruder, more direct and impatient style. Mine, says William James, 'being to say a thing in one sentence as straight and explicit as it can be made, and then to drop it forever; yours being to avoid naming it straight, but by dint of breathing and sighing all round and round it, to arouse in the reader who may have had a similar perception already (Heaven help him if he hasn't) the illusion of a solid object, made wholly out of impalpable materials, air, and the prismatic interferences of light, ingeniously focused by mirrors upon empty space.' But, he added, 'you *do* it, that's the queerness!'[16] That's the pragmatism, that's the greatness of variety: that things can be done in many ways. And yet William James sought, above all, to go not round and round but press forward in his prose, 'vehicular and transitive', to carry forward his sought-after meaning, leaving what got him there behind.[17]

He offers another great image for consciousness in this alternating double aspect:

> Like a bird's life, it seems to be made of an alternation of flights and perchings. The rhythm of language expresses this, where every thought is expressed in a sentence, and every sentence closed by a period. The resting-places are usually occupied by sensorial imaginations of some sort, whose peculiarity is that they can be held before the mind for an indefinite time, and contemplated without changing; the places of flight are filled with thoughts of relations, static or dynamic, that for the most part obtain between the matters contemplated in the periods of contemplative rest.
>
> (*PP* 1, p. 243, chapter 9, 'The Stream of Thought')

These achieved 'resting-places' are what James called the 'substantive parts'—the goals and conclusions achieved, the 'I' supposed to have achieved them. The 'places of flight' are the 'transitive [or transitional] places' in the process of thought. The basic aim of thinking is practical and teleological, to get from one landing place to another: 'The main end of our thinking is at all times the attainment of some other substantive part than the one from which we have just been dislodged' (*PP* 1, p. 243, chapter 9, 'The Stream of Thought'). We cannot stay for ever in mid-air, we have to get a hold on another branch. But so much depends on how far those mental perchings can incorporate what went into the flight towards them. James is not against the consolidation: it is in our nature to want to get somewhere, to need a solid result, even though only some of what was richly potential within the means gets released into the specific outcome this time round. Whenever there is some new contradictory find, the result is 'an inward trouble' to which a person's mind 'till then had been a stranger' and from which some refuge is sought by modifying the previous mass of experience. We can hardly help wanting whatever is new to be assimilated as far as possible with our old familiar stock of ideas and belief. We save as much as we can, 'for in this matter of belief we are all extreme conservatives' (*Pragmatism*, lecture 2, 'What Pragmatism Means').

That means there is always an excess of quality and feeling, perhaps serving for another time in the world. The words or actions we employ never wholly replace the implicit that prompted them: as Eugene Gendlin, another psychologist reader of James puts it, they 'carry the implying with them. They bring it. They carry it forward.' It is vital that 'the implying never fully turns into something explicit, as if it is now no longer there'.[18] It is still there, it is more than any end achieved, it is even what a person should love and represent. That is why any achieved end is best when not ignorant of its own inner biography or its own future potential to go on again.

In the next chapter I will turn back to the macro level of individual lives. For the moment I want to end by trying to explain again to myself why this grammar of William James is important and not just technical. Why aren't these little enabling words on the wing—'each', 'or', 'some', 'near', 'just gone'—merely trifling? It is because they are part of how this way of thinking overcomes stuckness—including the depression that characterized William

James in the years of trying to become William James twice-born—without even having to over-emphasize the issue. The seemingly negligible little words, hidden within the ordinary, are like the brain's accelerated short-cuts to where quality and potential are alive, always prior to the normalizing ego. These enabling particles, unsullied by over-consciousness, are not just grammatical but psychological; not just psychological but philosophical, and looking to be existentially translated into real-world stances and outcomes. They are waiting to be filled out. They mark the felt presence and the passage of the Implicit as part of our very reality. They attest to the existence of a silent meaningfulness between flights and rests and flights again, working in the interstitial spaces and the active gaps in ways not to be dropped but by somehow carried forward. Like clues, they begin to bespeak a different world view.

THE WILL TO BELIEVE

It was not only Walt Whitman who could write 'who touches this book touches a man':

> The books of all the great philosophers are like so many men. Our sense of an essential personal flavor in each one of them, typical but indescribable, is the finest fruit of our accomplished philosophic education.
>
> (*Pragmatism*, lecture 1, 'The Present Dilemma in Philosophy')

This doesn't mean that every point of view is 'only' subjective or every idea is 'really' nothing but psychological. It means that every deep intellectual or philosophical problem is simultaneously a psychological and ontological one, in its origins and its effects within the whole being of the individual.

Students may forget or not yet know this, James told them. They may work hard on working out the intricate details of a system, but when all the labour of understanding is done there remains something cruder that is nonetheless necessary—to see the wood for the trees as we say:

> the mind always performs its big summarizing act, and the system forthwith stands over against one like a living thing with that strange simple note of individuality which haunts our memory, like the wraith of man, when a friend or enemy of ours is dead.
>
> (*Pragmatism*, chapter 1, 'The Present Dilemma in Philosophy')

Humans will always need to do this, James believes: namely, get the overall human message at the macro level. And yet that rough gut intuition of a recognizable living entity is at the same time rightly said to be rather subtly indescribable. 'There is always a *plus*, a *thisness*, which feeling alone can answer for. Philosophy in this sphere is thus a secondary function' (VRE, p. 346, lecture 18, 'Philosophy'). The primary is this:

> You see now why I have been so individualistic throughout these lectures...
>
> Individuality is founded in feeling; and the recesses of feeling, the darker, blinder strata of character, are the only places in the world in which we catch the real fact in the making, and directly perceive how events happen, and how work is actually done.
>
> (VRE, p. 380, lecture 20, 'Conclusions')

You may be as refined and sophisticated and scrupulous as you can be in your thinking, but after that, 'I ask you in all seriousness to look abroad on the colossal universe of concrete facts, on their awful bewilderments, their surprises and cruelties, on the wildness which they show, and then to tell me whether "refined" is the one inevitable descriptive adjective that springs to your lips' (*Pragmatism*, lecture 1, 'The Present Dilemma in Philosophy'). For some nineteenth-century thinkers such as F. D. Maurice, there was a problem: 'There must be some way of uttering ourselves without talking about ourselves.'[1] But for James in his passionate salvos, this was no problem, this was the essence of thinking—not thinking of ourselves but incorporating those selves inside the thinking. Immersion in the 'wild' or 'bewildering': that is what 'in all seriousness' life demanded of thought, and that was what thought forced out of its thinker. Hence the need for something more raw that was to be found in the 'recesses' of individual feeling, beneath the dignified finish of most publications. Hence I offer here the pre-formal story of a visceral reader, an individual example back at the macro level.

*

The first time I think that anyone mentioned William James to me was at university in 1976. Naomi as I will call her was a graduate research student, further on than I was, who was studying psychology but reading a lot of philosophy alongside. She especially recommended the essays in the volume *The Will to Believe* as pieces of mental equipment for courage that she needed when she had no other counsel. She told me that she and her younger brother were the children of two survivors of the Holocaust. They had married each other in middle age, she said, because they felt there was no one else either could marry except someone who had known the Camps. But for just that reason it was an anxious and gloomy house without much laughter or touch. It was nonetheless to protect the children that the parents, who communicated secretly in Yiddish when they needed to, never spoke of what had happened to them. One day Naomi innocently brought home from infant school a book about the Holocaust, but before she could read it or talk about it, it simply disappeared. She told her younger brother whilst she was still only a little girl, 'We have to be happy, we must try to be *happy*. Because they are not.' It was one of the saddest things I have ever heard.

In secondary school, she said it was typical that she was the only one in her class who did not stay for school dinner but travelled home, with a quick turn-round time, before having to go all the way back again. She found she was clever, and would bring home news of her successes; but she felt she had to fight to do well, to over-revise so as to be safe for the exams. Even then, entering the exam room, she felt these fears of hers were comparatively small and shameful, childish and negligible. They could not matter enough, given what her parents must have gone through—which she couldn't help them with.

It is no surprise perhaps that, with that background, it was psychology she went on to study at university, though it had not been all she had hoped. But she loved thinking, as though books had to be in place of parents and guides. Sometimes she was so struck, she said, by an idea that it kept her awake at night with excitement. She related this to what play had been like for her as a child. If she loved some book or was thrilled by some TV programme, she would immediately create some physical drama-story out of it in which she could impersonate the leading figure. Riding a chair-arm as if it were a horse could keep the story going she said, giving it extension into a further pretend-world. But if somehow her acting-out didn't go right and she lost the plot, she would have to stop, with terrible frustrated sadness, and compulsively go all the way back to the beginning again. Now as a student she apologetically chain-smoked cigarettes, to stop and to re-channel that restless outer energy of hers, to help her sit still and think. William James, psychologist *and* philosopher, was an author who made her think better, whose ideas had been of help to her in making more of a human being out of herself.

She loved ideas. I thought of her again years after, when I read this image in James:

> Now let the water represent the world of sensible facts, and let the
> air above it represent the world of abstract ideas. Both worlds are
> real, of course, and interact; but they interact only at their bound-
> ary, and the locus of everything that lives, or happens to us, as far as

full experience goes, is the water. We are like fishes swimming in
the sea of sense, bounded above by the superior element, but unable
to breathe it pure or penetrate it.

(*Pragmatism*, lecture 4, 'The One and the Many')

Being immersed like fishes 'swimming in a sea of sense' is our
primordial condition, says James. Whatever the sublime ideas or
ideals, the cherished thoughts and memories above us, after coming
up for their air we have to return to our element, with whatever of
them we can keep for oxygen. 'The earth must resume its rights',
he wrote, its gravity plunging us back down into 'the very thick of
its sand and gravel', amidst 'the dirt of the world'.[2] And that return
to earth seemed welcome to Naomi, if she could take back with
her what she had found through thinking.

She said to me, as a student of literature, that because he wrote
in a literary style, James was considered neither a scientific psychologist nor a professional philosopher. Yet pursuing the largest
issues, he had said in *The Varieties of Religious Experience* that if you
simply asked people what is human life's chief concern, one of the
answers you'd always get back would be 'Happiness'. But then,
how to gain it, and keep it, and even recover it? 'We must try to be
happy': this promise had been neither achieved nor relinquished.
She knew happiness was a relative term, best known not as some
absolute state but even in the feeling of movement from the more
sad to the less so.

It is not for certain that we are determined by what went before.
That was one thing James meant to her. In that little space I want
to do what Chekhov says, she told me, 'Squeeze the slave out of
myself', and though obviously I value my education, my life can't
just be about having books to help me. If you have life, you should
make a life. She wanted eventually to have children of her own

and of course, do it differently from her parents, to see instead of the old depression some things happening for the first time, infants learning to say words like they were new, or telling you their secret thoughts. William James as a reader was, she said, good at getting to the human centre of what he read. He especially recommended a lesser-known essay by Robert Louis Stevenson entitled 'The Lantern-Bearers'. It was about Stevenson being a child and secretly carrying an inefficient tin lantern under his coat, to meet with other boys after school, towards nightfall, in some cold and muddy den where suddenly the lantern would make everything light. In the rude mound of mud there was a golden chamber. To an external observer the games they got up to in their den would have seemed nothing, and for Stevenson himself it was the journey there with the hidden lantern that was more important than its end. But it was for the poet-part of human beings to give a voice to what was really going on inside: 'For to miss the joy is to miss all. In the joy of the actors lies the sense of any action.' I later found that this was from James's lecture 'On a Certain Blindness in Human Beings'. But Naomi particularly mentioned 'The Will to Believe', to get at that 'needy bit' in yourself, she said, from which to make another go at life.

This is an incomplete story from forty years ago, one afternoon's long conversation, out of nowhere. She said that though normally it might sound too dramatic, hers was the story of an inner 'diaspora': parts of her scattered in various places, times, and people, looking for a new home. But psychology was the place to start from, because it held everything there in solution before it had to become anything else. When a mind becomes conscious of its own workings, it is already, she said, the psychologist to itself. The phrase was James's.[3]

I don't think we met much again, and certainly not to talk at that level. So I don't know what happened to this impressive person, and whether she made it, though she was vibrant and knew the fight ahead, and remains a powerful image. Nor did I go from her recommendation straight to the book and find there a dramatic revelation like hers.

It was only when much later I was by chance reading some William James essays in an Everyman selection that I came across 'The Will to Believe' and remembering the recommendation, went on to look for the whole volume of that title that contained further related pieces. And it was only after I began reading *The Will to Believe and Other Essays*, on and off, that a real memory of the meeting some three or four years earlier came back to me—in the midst of reading. It is important that it was that way round, in all the oddness of time, especially in relation to thinking and reading and remembering over a life.

I see now from my old notes and marks that three sentences are singled out, besides the one I mentioned in chapter 1 of this book. I would now, after Bion, call these sentences 'o', not only near the centre of William James, but William James near the very centre of a vital truth, and taking his readers there with him.

The first is about pessimism, doubt, lack of confidence, when you can't seem to try.

> Your mistrust of life has removed whatever worth your own enduring existence might have given to it. ('Is Life Worth Living?')

It is important it is a single sentence, made of (and here again I deploy pointing and counting) the relation between two thoughts. It would not be so powerful were they separate: Your existence can add to the meaning of life. Your mistrust takes the meaning away. '*Whatever*' is vital, if agnostic, in between. But there is still the pre-emptive maths: 'mistrust *removed*' whatever you '*might have given*'. You could never be neutral: you were either the adder or the subtractor, the person with confidence or doubt. For really on either side of the equation, James insists, 'both effort and resistance are ours' and we choose with which of the two to most identify our *selves* (PP 2, p. 576, chapter 26, 'The Will'). It is like what I remember of one of those first experiences of vital thought—when as a child you catch your own hand in a door and no one else is there to help: your painfully trapped hand has to be set free by the separate calm use of your other hand. '*Both* are ours.'

This is what the world is: if M equals the mass of mundane phenomena, says James in algebraic mode, then $M_1 + x$ represents the reaction of the individual thinker upon it, adding something to the good or to the bad, either way. The algebra is not inhuman. Naomi was always thinking how to get hold of the 'x' in her, to find out what it could do and how it could be accessed.

So on the other side of the equation, my two further heavily-marked sentences seized on what 'your enduring existence might have *given*' that the loss of your existence would have taken away:

> There are then cases, then, when a fact cannot come at all unless a preliminary faith exists in its coming. And *where faith in a fact can help create the fact*... ('The Will to Believe')
> And often enough our faith beforehand in an uncertified result is *the only thing that makes the result come true.* ('Is Life Worth Living?')

They came from what twenty-five years earlier, on 30 April 1870, had happened to William James when, amidst his own depression and on the verge of the abyss, he himself read one sentence in particular from the French philosopher, Renouvier, as his journal of the time testifies:

> I think that yesterday was a crisis in my life. I finished the first part of Renouvier's second *Essais* and see no reason why his definition of free will — 'the sustaining of a thought because I choose to when I might have other thoughts' — need be the definition of an illusion. At any rate, I will assume for the present — until next year — that it is no illusion. My first act of free will shall be to believe in free will.
>
> (Perry, p. 121)

'Assume for the present — it is no illusion' is still frail, and the bootstrapping formulation that the first act of free will shall be to believe *in* free will feels almost a self-conscious confidence trick. Yet what I read in James's essays felt different from their original in the journal, less merely hopeful but consolidated now: 'faith *in* a fact can help *create* the fact'; 'our faith *beforehand* in an *uncertified* result is the *only* thing that *makes* the result *come true*'. Something in the new tightness of the syntax clinched it: you can believe in something before it exists, which would not subsequently exist if you had not believed in it. The struggle of the syntax to get it the right way round, in formulations improvised in the very course of writing and thinking, was like someone trying to work on his or her own brain. James's student and first biographer, Ralph Perry gets it right when he rewords the journal-entry in the spirit of the later essays, in this shape: 'To believe *by* an act of will *in* the efficacy *of* the will.'[4]

I have read and re-read these sentences of James's and every time they do something, serving almost literally to re-mind, in the way that a line of poetry might:

> 'I came to that place in the poem,' as a friend said to me once, 'and clunk! my mind turned inside out, quite painlessly. "Huh?" I said,

and read that bit again, and it happened again, precisely there, and I couldn't explain it to myself.'[5]

There! says the pointer, 'o' to steer by. For there, out of all the possible formulations, is the one ('clunk!') of which we feel *It fits*. And not because it merely fits *in* with pre-existing assumptions: on the contrary the fit is a surprise, a burst of recognition for a writer who deliberately ranges across subject areas and disciplines, who himself refuses to be a neat fit into any one category but relishes the diverse mix. So if whatever it is fits in that way, it fits *what*? Fits something in the writer, fits something in the reader, but above all fits with something they sense in the reality of the world. We don't have to know—because we cannot know—immediately what it fits with, why it 'works' or feels 'right'; but what we can do is try to follow it, its implications and resonances, in further thoughts and through further sentences.

Such is the effect of that 'feeling of *if*', creating a space for human intervention, in another essay in the volume, 'The Sentiment of Rationality'. There James says this—only before I start, I want to warn you that I shall be quoting it bit by bit, interrupting the wonderful forward flow of his sentence, through what Robert Frost calls its 'straight crookedness', by inserting pointers and adding line-endings to count the thoughts in their turning clauses. So here it goes:

> *If* then the proof exist not till I have acted
> *and* I must needs in acting run the risk of being wrong

—'*how*' on earth, he then goes on—and James's work is pretty much done by the time he is ending this—how on earth can those rationalists demand I do nothing until complete evidence of doing right is provided in advance?

And then he goes again, back to the 'if', fighting for its right to move out of subordination:

> *If* this really be a moral universe
> *if* by my acts I be a factor of its destinies
> *if* to believe where I may doubt be itself a moral act
> analogous to voting for a side *not yet* sure to win —
> *by what right* shall they close in upon me
> *and* steadily negate the deepest conceivable function of my being...?

Negate the *deepest!*—and to finish off the sentence again as it moves just past 'o': 'By what right do those critics negate my being through their literally "preposterous" demand that I move no muscle but somehow remain forever balancing myself in irresolvable doubt?'

It feels wonderful, that pulse in these sentences before they close into final sense; the musical counterpoint in the productive tension between their forward drive and the retarding insistences of what morally must have a place in the world. 'If this be really a moral universe...'. It makes the word 'moral' exciting and real and fighting again—in a moral universe, to believe a moral act. 'If by my acts I be a factor of [that universe's] destinies...'. James writes it such that within the 'fact', there is still oneself as a potential 'factor', in act, working towards its possible destinies and destinations. Sometimes you have to force a gap ('by what right shall they close in upon me?'), and then 'to fill it up is our thought's destiny' (PP 1, p. 259, chapter 9, 'The Stream of Thought'). For me these seem no longer abstract words but more like the mental equivalent of muscle memories, as Renouvier's sentence was for James. They stir something that cannot quite be remembered as one specific event. James had read and admired John Henry Newman's *Apologia Pro Vita Sua* (1864), marking sundry key points in the man's slow and painful movement from the Anglican to the

Catholic Church. But there is especially this passage on the idea of 'indescribable' process:

> For who can know himself, and the multitude of subtle influences which act upon him? and who can recollect, at the distance of twenty-five years, all that he once knew about his thoughts and his deeds, and that, during a portion of his life, when even at the time his observation, whether of himself or of the external world, was less than before or after, by very reason of the perplexity and dismay which weighed upon him...
>
> (*Apologia Pro Vita Sua*, Part V, 'History of
> My Religious Opinions, 1839–1841')

There was no one moment of clear revelation; it was what Newman after the Greeks called 'lysis' rather than 'crisis', a gradual rather than an abrupt recovery from sickness (VRE, p. 145, chapter 8, 'The Divided Self'). Eventually, through a long period of shapelessness he had found his mind in a new place—but how? Can't fully recollect now; did not clearly know then; but it surfaced as a ratification of a change that had already virtually, implicitly happened. This is a deep illustration of James's point about the hidden places of transition we can barely register even from within the passage of our own experience. 'Certain causes too minute for our apprehension' may at a certain moment 'tip' our destiny 'one way or another' (*PP 1*, p. 139, chapter 5, 'The Automaton Theory'). That elusive but emphatic experience is, I am saying as a reader, what James's writing almost physically summons the feel of: the felt presence almost at the level of the nervous system of 'this dumb region of the heart where we dwell alone with our willingnesses and unwillingnesses, our faiths and fears' ('Is Life Worth Living?').

Out of it, for me, hundreds of James's other thoughts seem to come tumbling, as if through cracking the safe of that deep inner region. It was first opened for him by Renouvier saying that freewill exists above all as 'the sustaining of a thought because I choose to, when I might have other thoughts'. And those insistent Jamesian feelings of 'if' mark just that attempt at sustaining of a thought 'when' otherwise I might have others more easily. For *if* freewill does exist, says James, it is not in the abstract but in 'the operation of free effort' which in practice 'could only be to hold some one ideal object, or part of an object a little longer or a little more intensely before the mind. (PP 2, p. 576, chapter 26, 'Will'). *Only…a little, a little*, is the inner cry. But if A naturally matters to us more than Z, and yet we know Z to be in the longer term more important, then 'only' the feeling of increased voluntary attention to Z by dint of extra effort can give Z any chance of prevailing against the line of least resistance. It is no use telling us to wait for all the rational evidence before making a decision, for decisions as to giving more or less attention are being made by us at some level all the time. 'Man needs a rule for his will', says James in 'The Sentiment of Rationality', where he means by 'rule' something that gives it allowance and scope, and not just enforces prohibition: 'Man needs a rule for his will, and will invent one if one be not given him.' That is the best tonal meaning of 'will'—not as the uptight noun in 'the will to believe' or the 'rule for his will'—but as embedded in the enabling auxiliary verb '*will* invent'—will just have to, incorrigibly, irrepressibly, willy-nilly, will invent whatever is needed when not given or if not allowed. Eventually must and will, somehow, sometime, somewhere; can't but.

Humans at their own risk have a right not to be vetoed as to what they need, and a right to believe in trying for it. Otherwise what they need will only take its revenge on them for its neglect, by ending in depression or bitterness. Our urgent needs and wants and feelings, seeking their way in the world, make so-called pragmatism closer to idealism-in-action. 'I can believe in the ideal as an ultimate, not as an origin, and as an extract, not the whole' (*Pragmatism*, lecture 8, 'Pragmatism and Religion').

> Nothing could be more absurd than to hope for the definitive triumph of any philosophy which should refuse to legitimate, and to legitimate in an emphatic manner, the more powerful of our emotional and practical tendencies.
>
> ('The Sentiment of Rationality')

We have feelings *about* feelings. A human being joys in reacting 'with such emotions as fortitude, hope, rapture, admiration, earnestness' but is very unhappy to have to react 'with fear, disgust, despair, or doubt': any human philosophy that would seek to legitimate the latter at the expense of the former can never survive, says James, because it does not fit with what we are. For to miss the joy is to miss all.

At the same time as our asserted right to try, there is even so a rather beautifully concessive willingness as well as will in it: 'I find myself willing to take the universe to be really dangerous and adventurous…I am willing that there should be real losses and real losers, and no preservation of all that is' (*Pragmatism*, lecture 8, 'Pragmatism and Religion'). But still humans are to be *fighters* for ends which without their lonely fight would not exist at all (PP 1, p. 141, chapter 5, 'The Automaton Theory'). As Naomi said to her brother, 'We must be happy, we must *try* to be happy':

> Of course we measure ourselves by many standards. Our strength and our intelligence, our wealth and even our good luck, are things which warm our heart and make us feel ourselves a match for life. But deeper than all such things, and able to suffice unto itself without them, is the sense of the amount of effort we can put

forth....Effort seems to belong to an altogether different realm, as if it were the substantive thing which we *are*, and those were but externals which we *carry*.   (PP 2, p. 578, chapter 26, 'Will')

Effort is the difference, inserting action into existence. 'He who can make none is but a shadow; he who can make much is a hero.'

'Hero' may not seem a useful word to us now. But given his love of life's plurality, and leaving aside for a moment the issue of gendered pronouns, James goes on to say that heroism occurs whenever the world finds in an individual its worthy match or mate, like a representative of the species leaping into some gap in reality, to undertake an inferred duty or responsibility. Then he or she is one who can '*stand* this universe', 'meet it', 'keep up faith in it', 'still find a zest in it'—and even more:

> just as our courage is so often a reflex of another's courage, so our faith is apt to be...a faith in someone else's faith. We draw new life from the heroic example.   (PP 2, p. 579, chapter 26, 'Will')

New life as if from the example of William James and his exuberance. And just so brother Henry learnt from him the ending of *The Ambassadors* (1903), summarized again in its Preface, when the ageing man at last says to the young one, so urgently and poignantly:

> 'Live all you can; it's a mistake not to. It doesn't so much matter what you do in particular so long as you have your life. If you haven't had that what *have* you had? I'm too old—too old at any rate for what I see. What one loses one loses; make no mistake about that. Still, we have the illusion of freedom; therefore don't, like me to-day, be without the memory of that illusion. I was either, at the right time, too stupid or too intelligent to have it, and now I'm a case of reaction against the mistake. Do what you like so long as you don't make it. For it *was* a mistake. Live, live!'

'Believe that life is worth living, and your belief will help create the fact.' Finally, belief or illusion, the novelist gets it out straight.

*

But Ralph Perry got it right when he said that what extraordinarily James needed to save him had to be a *philosophy*—to create a state of mind (a capacity for thinking and a psychology to accompany it) that could convert by re-description a doubt into a chance, and in which faith *is* faith because doubt is still possible. The philosophy came out of the prepositions, the shorthand signs of 'my' efforts to do something with or make something of 'myself', as human beings begin to see it as their part to try, themselves, to add to the world what they find lacking in it. As if the lacking was their clue and cue. Then it is astonishing that 'facts' are things that can 'be made' and 'created', and not just found obdurate.

This is not just the therapeutic exhortations of 'self-help' or 'positivity', 'optimism', or 'healthy mindedness', names that are like inert and past things; but rather something that gets under the skin, behind the forehead, and shows its present passage there. It is the very shape of such an idea as registered in its twisting, looping syntax, mirrored in the nervous system, which makes imaginable and thus possible a sense of the inner mental gymnastics required to put it into use.

But James's is a world that is 'always vulnerable': having no permanent reassurances, a thinker within it 'must always feel to some degree insecure' (*The Meaning of Truth*, chapter 11, 'The Absolute and the Strenuous Life'). 'To some *degree*' is itself a key phrase, when it is said of the thing sought in one mood, grammatical as well as psychological, that in the form of doubt it *may* be, but in the form of possibility it still may *be*.

> Not a victory is gained, not a deed of faithfulness or courage is
> done, except upon a maybe; not a service, not a sally of generosity,
> not a scientific exploration or experiment or text-book, that may
> not be a mistake.   ('Is Life Worth Living?')

That is the force of 'up-on' ('no victory gained except upon a
maybe') as the preposition of precariously weighed dependency;
the knife-edge of a decision that can never be fully thought
through but only lived out. But beneath the 'maybe' is something
that a maybe can never blithely dismiss, 'our troubles lie too deep':

> The fact that we *can* die, that we *can* be ill at all, is what perplexes us;
> the fact that we now for a moment live and are well is irrelevant to
> that perplexity. We need a life not correlated with death, a health
> not liable to illness, a kind of good life that will not perish, a good
> in fact that flies beyond the Goods of nature.
>
> (VRE p. 113, lecture 6, 'The Sick Soul')

In James' grammar of life that 'can be' is a built-in condition.
Present happiness, like a form of luck, may not finally ignore that.
And what we 'need', a life without death, a health without illness,
is not able to dismiss it. All that the need can do, to maintain a version of itself and not be haplessly defeated, is to try to put the
threat, the liability and the perplexity into a place that is almost
bearable. That is the human reason for something always psychologically like religion, even when religion seems past.

The philosophy I defend, wrote James, 'has to fall back on a certain ultimate hardihood, a certain willingness to live without
assurances or guarantees' (*The Meaning of Truth*, chapter 11, 'The
Absolute and the Strenuous Life'). But what is there to fall back
upon, when coming out of a childhood of traumatic gloom and
insecurity such as Naomi's, for example? Imagine a more explicit

god, is James's response, as he offers the thought-experiment of this unrefined invitation:

> Suppose that the world's author put the case to you before creation, saying: 'I am going to make a world not certain to be saved, a world the perfection of which shall be conditional merely, the condition being that each several agent does its own "level best". I offer you the chance of taking part in such a world. Its safety, you see, is unwarranted. It is a real adventure, with real danger, yet it may win through. It is a social scheme of co-operative work genuinely to be done. Will you join the procession? Will you trust yourself and trust the other agents enough to face the risk?'
>
> (*Pragmatism*, lecture 8, 'Pragmatism and Religion')

It is precisely what is missing: an almost impossible and certainly paradoxical meta-assurance that it is alright to have no assurances here. And yet it is still only 'as if' a god said it; the 'suppose' is only another greater 'maybe' to encourage further ones. 'We can act *as if* there were a God; feel *as if* we were free' (VRE, p. 49, lecture 3, 'The Reality of the Unseen'), where 'as if' is like the very beginning of imagination arising out of ordinary human needs and intuitions. But Naomi came from parents who no longer believed in God after what had happened to them. What happens to those who want in some way to trust or to believe, knowing its value, but cannot? Or, to those who, made hopeless by their lack of agency, seem to settle into just being okay, nothing special, with nothing much to complain of—not even despairing but, as Kierkegaard put it in *The Sickness Unto Death*, despairing of despair?

For James, *wanting* to believe is actually closer to belief than we think. But we will hardly realize that, when we want courage even to believe that courage itself is possible. What we need in order to get that nascent 'something' to start from, and break the vicious circle, is what James in 'The Will to Believe' calls 'precursive faith', the launch-pad for 'maybe' and 'as if', ahead of evidence and doubt.

It comes out of a theological concept. James' philosophy was, he sometimes said, a descendant of the Protestant Reformation, that shift in world-view which freed the struggling individual of whatever background from the mediating institutions of the Catholic Church.[6] For the reformers stood for 'powers which even the meanest of men might carry with them – faith and self-despair – but which were personal, requiring no priestly intermediation, and brought their owner face to face with God' ('The Sentiment of Reality'). But how is a lonely, doubting, guilty individual to rescue faith from self-despair? James's 'precursive faith' derives from the doctrine of 'prevenient grace', particularly vital to the psychology of Protestant individualism. For as the name suggests, prevenient grace precedes the grace of God by disposing human beings to be able to shun their own hardened guilt and hopelessness, and accept a mercy and forgiveness they know to be unmerited. George Herbert's poem 'Love III' shows how hard such acceptance can be when Love in the form of Christ comes to the poem's protagonist like a welcoming host: 'yet my soul drew back / Guilty of dust and sin'. His soul flinches, the man cannot come home, he cannot cross the threshold—though quick-eyed Love, seeing his reluctance, 'Drew nearer to me, sweetly questioning, / If I lacked any thing':

> A guest, I answered, worthy to be here:
>   Love said, You shall be he.
> I the unkind, ungrateful? Ah my dear,
>   I cannot look on thee.
> Love took my hand, and smiling did reply,
>   Who made the eyes but I?

Truth Lord, but I have marred them: let my shame
Go where it doth deserve.
And know you not, says Love, who bore the blame?

Christ bore the blame by his sacrifice. So it was even from our mythic beginning with Adam and Eve immediately following the Fall:

Thus they, in lowliest plight, repentant stood
Praying; for from the mercy-seat above
Prevenient grace descending had removed
The stony from their hearts, and made new flesh
Regenerate grow instead… (Milton, *Paradise Lost*, 11, 1–5)

Prevenient grace turns the hardened stone back to vulnerable flesh. It predisposes the fallen human race to be able to want and receive what, unbearably, they know they do not deserve, and cannot earn, and desperately need.

Never mind if you think you do not believe in such things, no matter even if you believe religion is precisely what used to produce such damning guilt. Before they know it and reject it, the William James of *The Varieties of Religious Experience* wants his readers to have the inner experience of something that had humanly existed in the world, as a *given* regardless of how or when or why. To be found in these crises of faith and despair was serious human data, not to be simply denounced or explained away, but re-imagined psychologically, even by a form of modern translation, such as 'prevenient grace' made over into 'precursive faith'.

It is this agnostic sense in William James of the givenness of things, of pragmatically, not dogmatically, adapting language and thought to best registering what is there, that attracts another of his great readers, the novelist Marilynne Robinson.[7] For what she values is the empirical mid-way position he holds, and keeps alive for thought, between firm believers and utter non-believers. Still writing within the Protestant tradition, but in a literary language that moves between worlds, across domains and ages, in all the richness of all possible meaning and implication, the novelist takes the term prevenient grace and extends it through the ageing minister John Ames in Robinson's *Gilead* (2004). 'I think', he writes, 'there must also be a prevenient courage that allows us to be brave – to acknowledge that there is more beauty than our eyes can bear...' (p. 280). But the man in despair who most needs such prevenience in the Gilead sequence of novels is Jack Boughton, the wastrel son of another minister, Ames's best friend. 'Hope', says Jack in *Home* (2008), 'is the worst thing in the world'; it makes a fool of you while it lasts:

> 'And then when it is gone there is nothing left for you at all. Except' — he shrugged and laughed — 'except what you can't be rid of.' (p. 286)

James would know that 'feeling of *except*' which sometimes saves but here only keeps the man alive, still agonizingly unable to feel nothing. There is also 'the feeling of *what*'—'what you can't get rid of': some incorrigible life at core that Jack can only have the wrong way round as burden not basis. Jack, in his guilt and shame, is one who cannot believe in his own capacity to change, cannot accept he is worthy of love or forgiveness, cannot bear to hope or to explain; but can only take refuge in rueful irony or hapless apology. He can scarcely avoid acts of self-damage, to keep away the people whom he fears he might otherwise hurt in their very efforts to care for him. Instead of the prevenient hope James might want for what he calls in *Varieties of Religious Experience* 'the sick soul', Jack wryly describes the life he has led as 'prevenient death' (*Jack*, 2020, p. 250)—as if, self-condemned, he has already known purgatory, on earth. What is a soul? his younger sister asks him in that purgatory he lives in. 'On the basis of my vast learning and experience', he says again with that defensive irony of his, 'I would say—it is what you can't get rid of' (*Home*, p. 300). That is the 'what' that Bion's o points to, at bottom.

I am saying that for a soul to survive, it is above all that seed of precursive faith—that prevenient courage and prevenient hope against depression and despair—which James aims to inspire in his writing. And for this purpose: that humans may be able to begin again, from even the lowest ebb, to manage something in this world.

And James must do that psychologically, in what often seems a post-religious age. He must recall the inner psyche of these old needs in what seemed to Naomi, in her terms, a diaspora—a scattering from any sense of centre or home, without a firm theology or philosophy to guide us, and sometimes without our even wanting one.

But here is the ending to the period of my reading that this chapter has tried to describe.

In 1981, at about the time I was beginning to read William James though seemingly unconnected to that, I noted in the Sunday papers an adverse review of a book about to come out, a book that the reviewer suggested was a doom-laden account of modern incoherence and confusion in the face of how to live life. I wanted to read that book at once, out of an intense awareness of what Thomas Hardy's *Jude the Obscure* had called 'a chaos of principles', and out of a feeling that the book might be a way to 'get at' something wrong that needed to be got right. The following Monday I did what I had never done before and never have since: I took a train to London, to the publishers, Duckworth, in the Old Piano Factory and got myself a copy of Alasdair MacIntyre's *After Virtue*, half of which I read hurriedly on the long train-journey back to Liverpool.

It is a book about Babel, or about Diaspora, the catastrophic scattering of any coherent world-view into fragments. MacIntyre said that it was as though all the great traditions, theologies, and philosophies, had been lodged in single surviving copies in the world's great library, and that library had then burnt down. All that was left us was charred bits and pieces, without foundations or proper order, with lost contexts and missing connections. That was what the modern mind was like, he thought: a mess of half-understood instincts, unexamined lessons, left-over messages, and confused conflicts. It fitted my sense of things at that time, the chaos of principles.

But I don't think that that now is what I want to say. Or rather the point or centre of orientation has moved. MacIntyre seemed to want the renewal of a coherent *tradition*, a fresh synthesis of lost ways of thinking, or otherwise (what seemed barely possible) some radical new start. But he was interested also in the more limited idea of what he called *practices*. These, though limited and temporary, passed on their own coherent rules and goals, had their own field of endeavour: as in football or chess or craft-making. But the best practices were those that not only had their internal rationale (such as what made for the function of a good footballer, chess-player, cabinet-maker) but an external value too (why should football or chess or furniture be significant under the eye of eternity?).

My life has been based in literary practice, which cannot exist wholly by itself because of all within it that has reference to outside. And what literary thinking has enabled me to do is think of MacIntyre's chaos and catastrophe in other terms—terms that, I now want to say, are closer to those I have been grateful to find increasingly through William James. It is literature that has provided an experimental, experiential holding-ground for all the mess that actually James himself also rather loved about human beings: the half-forgotten faith or ill-applied principles, the emotions and memories and ideas, the botches and pains and excitements, the searches and the too-brief revelations. It is a holding-ground but also a melting pot: every time in reading and writing and thinking, it means having 'to some degree' to have to start over, with whatever it is that has to be lived out this time, with whatever of the old equipment that can be adapted and reused, or must be questioned and subsumed. I have studied not only books but also other people, like Naomi here. People, that is to say, who equivalently have been reading for life, without the assurance of prior explanations, or with their prior defaults made vulnerable. Readers working away at thinking in the making, not knowing in advance, but taking literature's venture as a second chance to think, translate, do over. That has been my own line and venture, and even amidst conflict it has offered a series of sudden and specific givens—thoughts and feelings of life, expressed in books and in responses to books—with which to work.

With William James, if there are different potentialities, there are different lives that help make them known, and those different people should talk to one another, in a sort of republic of collaborative thinking that represents more of the spectrum of human potential than any one individual can manage alone.

> The notion of 'partaking' has a deep and real significance. Whoso partakes of a thing enjoys his share, and comes into contact with the thing and its other partakers. But he claims no more.... Why may not the world be a sort of republican banquet of this sort, where all the qualities of being respect one another's personal sacredness, yet sit at the common table of space and time?
> ('On Some Hegelisms')

Why otherwise so many possibilities and points of view? Part, partial, part-takers: those are his terms in place of wholes and totals and absolutes. The variety must be *for* something, for 'why, if one act of knowledge could from one point take in the total perspective, with all mere possibilities abolished, should there ever have been anything more than that act?' ('On Some Hegelisms'). *There* was James' boredom: why should a plan of creation serve merely to duplicate that one whole view, tediously, again and again, life after life? He inferred a different plan: 'On the other hand, if we stipulate only a partial community of partially independent powers, we see perfectly why no one part controls the whole view, but each detail must come and be actually given' ('On Some Hegelisms').

> The first three notes of a tune comport many endings, all melodious, but the tune is not named till a particular ending has actually come... ('On Some Hegelisms')

There was no one tune or guaranteed ending. There were different thoughts at different times in one life and in different forms across many lives. America's democratic republic was the model for a modern society of human variety, experiment and untidied diversity. That is why during the writing of this book I am thinking about William James with the aid of people both present and past, reading him with fellow-readers.

The demanding power of this literary-like practice means, however, that this is not just about living meekly with incoherence and uncertainty, comfortably pluralistic across the whole range of the possible and plausible, in what is too often called after Keats 'negative capability'. It is more like positive incapability in which you still have to do something. It has positively to do with the narrowing-down of making a choice and taking a chance; with unavoidable risk and risky belief; with partial perspective and attempted action. It is to do with being affected by thoughts coming from anywhere that have their own life for you as instruments of potential being—and going with them, without immediate recognition of explicit origin, or specific ownership, or clear direction.

The thoughts themselves are like an inner congregation even in a single mind, says my James. On any one occasion, in any trial, one thought may feel itself the successor of another, carrying forwards its purpose, or may find that for now it is blocked and superseded. Go with what you can. There is, as James variously describes it, a felt warmth between different mental elements as though they were cognizant of each other; a suddenly perceived intimacy, or a magnetic belonging together; a past feeling 'receiving the greeting' of a present thought; a sense of vibrations and reverberations 'striving with or against, saying yes or no', along various cross-cutting 'lines of direction' in the mind's brain.[8] Each pulse of consciousness knows and feels its predecessor already within itself, passing on the continuous claims of identity and ownership, of change and adaption. It is as though internally within the nervous system one thought or moment of being speaks to another, finding it more or less warm, at its warmest greeting it by signalling: 'Thou art *mine*, and part of the same self with me':

> Each Thought is both an owner, and dies owned, transmitting whatever it realized as its Self to its later proprietor.
>
> (*PP* 1, p. 339, chapter 10, 'The Consciousness of Self')

This is what 'me' is: not some separately knowable entity called Self, but whatever makes the warm connection, or feels the shock of difference, or knows it is in neutral, registering the psychological temperature-changes, as experience goes on along the horizontal. I love this on-going sense of something which, within all that, recognizes, constitutes and re-organizes me, like antennae, as I go along. Woe betide me if I try to name or define it, and say what it *is* outside its work; but woe betide me also if I ignore what it *does*, what it says through its messages and its alarms, in all that ceaseless monitoring so sensitive to the movements of a life:

> Some experiences simply abolish their predecessors without continuing them in any way. Others are felt to increase or to enlarge their meaning, to carry out their purpose, or to bring us nearer to their goal. They 'represent' them, and may fulfil their function better than they fulfilled it themselves.
>
> (*The Meaning of Truth*, chapter 4, 'The Relation between Knower and Known')

And so it goes on across the conjunctions and disjunctions of James' mental grammar: this network of a self almost constantly re-forming, in the effort to survive and prosper. For better or for worse, what is 'me' and 'mine' expands and contracts, half-blindly fights off the forward consequence of one past, or seeks a better future for another.

And still experience keeps making calls and claims upon that self, however much it wants to stay safe and fixed and separate. In this demand for entry, thoughts become for James what in that last passage, on the relation between knower and known, he wonderfully calls *representatives*. Representatives, that is to say, of diverse times, people, situations, moods, meanings, chances, even different worlds and realities: transmissions seeking a host in which to become re-activated. James insists, in celebration: 'Why, after all, may not the world be so complex as to consist of many interpenetrating spheres of reality, which we can thus approach in alternation...? (*VRE*, p. 100, lecture 4, 'The Religion of Healthy Mindedness'). Across that complex world of many dimensions and persons, thoughts are 'dynamogenic agents, or stimuli for unlocking what would otherwise be unused reservoirs of individual power' ('The Energies of Men'). Those agents and representatives look in this newer vision of mental reality to become people and actions.

I turn in the next chapter to consider further that mental network we carry around us, which James called a 'field' of consciousness.

JAMES'S FIELD WORK

Sometimes it happens the other way round. It's not always that you consciously know you have a problem, and then find a direct and relevant solution to it. But rather you may hear or read something, and it *fits*, shifting something you hadn't quite known was wrong, as if sub-conscious and conscious had now suddenly clicked into place together, in release of tension. Before that, you may not have fully realized, or couldn't acknowledge, that there *was* a problem. And not always out of denial, pride or fear; but because you didn't know that it could ever be different or solvable. Then the consciousness of it would only seem to make it worse. Reading William James can be that sort of experience: his giving what you hadn't previously realized you had lacked or wanted.

But then suppose no solution ever came along. The great novella 'The Beast in the Jungle' was written by Henry James almost immediately after he had read his brother's *Varieties of Religious Experience*. It concerns the strange psychology of an ageing man, John Marcher, who spends his life thinking that something tragically terrible is destined to happen to him. Only, as his female companion begins to realize, the terrible thing is that, actually, nothing will ever 'happen' to him at all. May Bartram knows Marcher suffers from a lack of ordinary human feeling. And when in her last illness he asks her what she has seen in him that clearly makes her fear for his future, what can she tell him? He is naturally blind to his emotional inadequacy, and perhaps that is a sort of terrible blessing. For even if she could make him see, what was the use at this late point? To take in the sense of a life wholly wasted, even were he capable of it, would be a near-killing realization.

You may not know what you have in you, and you may not know what you lack. Instead of such knowledge of what we are or are not capable of, there is only *pragmatism*, the testing and the trying, and the bare result. And still what gets lost or left out or neglected along the way is usually obliterated within the individual outcome. 'We don't come to our own': 'It is there but we don't get at it' ('The Energies of Men'). This chapter begins with 'it', that strange potential that is hard to get at.

These thoughts about what is not there, or is there but not known to be, are retrospectively the background to an apparently minor little passage I recently re-read from William James's *The Meaning of Truth*, feeling again the temporal strangeness I had felt when first I came upon it.

It is about Ursa Major, the Great Bear, and the pattern of stars within it. Seven stars within the wider constellation came to be called, variously, the big dipper or the plough. 'We say', wrote James, 'they were seven before they were counted': their shape, in some resemblance to a wagon or a plough or a long-handled cup, already existed before any one ever actually perceived it. Then James asks a mind-staggering question: 'But what do we mean by this projection into past eternity of recent human ways of thinking?'

> Were they explicitly seven, or explicitly bear-like, before the human witness came? Surely nothing in the truth of the attributes drives us to think this. They were only implicitly or virtually what we call

them, and we human witnesses first explicated them and made them 'real'. A fact virtually pre-exists when every condition of its realization save one is already there.

(*The Meaning of Truth*, chapter 3 'Humanism and Truth')

'Save one': the presence of humans to name 'things'.

I don't have much interest in astronomy. But this example of James's seemed suddenly important and helpful, not for its information but more indirectly, as connected to what I said just now: about a solution retrospectively revealing a barely acknowledged problem in the very act of dispelling it. In particular, the word 'virtual' meant more than I had known before, as if it enabled some sort of insertion of thought into the otherwise closed-up nature of reality. But what was the word doing, what was this passage speaking to? It was that way round, trying to think backwards.[1] One thing I did know was that it wasn't merely abstract or intellectual, however much it looked like that. It felt psychological, strangely equivalent to some sort of therapeutic breakthrough.

James could *either* have written that reality was complete and ready-made, the seven stars just hanging there patiently waiting, as it were, for our intellects to register their existence. *Or*, conversely, he might have said that the naming of the plough was only a human fiction arbitrarily projected upon an unmeaning universe, to give it some false and fanciful anthropomorphic order. But I always hate it whenever I get stuck in this territory of mutually weakening alternatives: no good whichever of the two you assent to, something has got split and cheapened. Instead, James's reformulations of what reality is are beautiful in the way a mathematical equation can be elegant, by putting things a wholly different way round, giving them an extra dimension that relieves both intellectual and psychological tension. So James described the astronomical discovery as if it were nearer to the experience of paradox:

> Undeniably something comes by the counting that was not there before. And yet that something was *always true*. In one sense you create it, and in another sense you *find* it.... In all such cases, odd as it may sound, our judgment may actually be said to retroact and enrich the past.
>
> (*The Meaning of Truth*, chapter 3, 'Humanism and Truth')

That was the strange recursive loop working between finding *and* making. 'Odd as it may sound', what was there beforehand and what was discovered now almost simultaneously realized each other, instead of the simple linear sequence of one being prior cause and the other being after-effect. To say that our thought does not just 'make' this reality, unilaterally, means

> that if our own particular thought were annihilated the reality would still be there in some shape, though possibly it might be a shape that would lack something that our thought supplies.
>
> (*The Meaning of Truth*, chapter 3, 'Humanism and Truth')

And when people say that reality is 'independent' of us, it means 'there is something in every experience that escapes our arbitrary control' ('Humanism and Truth'). How beautifully tentative and respectful James is with both the coming-in of 'possibly it might be...lack[ing] something our thought supplies' and the going-out of 'something in every experience...escapes'. But it remains mentally dizzying: that the stars were there independently *before* you recognized them, but even that 'before' was in another sense *not* there *until* you recognized them. Time could turn around within itself.

These strange relations can't quite be seen or grasped or entirely abstracted: though they feel *like* thought, they can't even quite *be* thought. The seven stars had been both there and not there, in different senses: they were what James calls 'virtual', existing before human discovery, in a kind of potent darkness. 'The object of every thought, then, is neither more nor less than all that the thought thinks, exactly as thought thinks it' (PP 1, p. 276). The original naming of 'the Plough' was not merely a labelling of what was already there, but had to do with everything that went into the creating of the thought as it first got made, how it brought world and mind together.

That re-joining-together of our reality happens again in a different way in the manuscript for a book on 'the Many and the One' that James never completed. It comes when James writes of what we call 'Time' and what we call 'Space'—the great receptacles in which the many sequences and co-existences of the world find order. These great forms, now taken for granted as common sense, together constitute one of those 'conceptions at once so antedulivian and so easy that we never think of them as the positive historic achievements they really must have been'.[2] But if only, suggests James, we could imagine an ancient people first needing and discovering them, bringing them into the world to better register what felt otherwise a chaos: that was the achievement, and that is the memory that has gone to sleep in us. Of such fundamental conceptions we just do not remember how 'each of them must once have been an invention' (MEN, p. 8). There are of course advantages to the settling down of knowledge—to use and build upon what does not have to be constantly reinvented but releases energy for further endeavours. But what James loves is that sudden re-discovery of an idea that has fossilized, which is like a renewal of the mind meeting the world. It finds again the potential within what otherwise had settled into the merely actual.

These are philosophical examples of original thinking, in the sense of recovering the very origins of the thought. But they can also take on human form. James lost his father in December 1882, his mother had died in the January, while his second son had been born midway between in the June. During his father's final illness, William was on a research trip in Europe. Brother Henry, the novelist, had urged him not to return home precipitately, and instead William sent his father a letter of farewell. It arrived too late, but Henry quietly read it aloud at the funeral, by the grave-side, as if their dead father could hear it. William then began editing a selection of his father's work, his *Literary Remains* which finally appeared in December 1884 as William's first book and his father's last. William's third son, Herman, had been born at the beginning of that year but died in July 1885. Again William had been busy with his work, especially when his wife was put into isolation, quarantined with scarlet fever a few months earlier, and the children had gone to her mother. Looking back he felt he had hardly known or seen that barely 18-month-old son. It was only in 1907 in *Pragmatism* that he wrote:

> To anyone who has ever looked on the face of a dead child or parent the mere fact that matter could have taken for a time that precious form, ought to make matter sacred ever after. It makes no difference what the *principle* of life may be, material or immaterial ... That beloved incarnation was among matter's possibilities.
>
> (*Pragmatism*, chapter 3, 'Some Metaphysical Problems Pragmatically Considered')

There the pragmatism was fully humanized, dismissing any abstract discussion of the rival principles of materialism and idealism. Instead there comes at the end of a life a first thought about the very nature of existence, personally experienced as if for the first time again. Possibility incarnated, matter taking beloved form, and then gone.

These are thoughts in perhaps their best form, as great bursting discoveries or re-discoveries. One of the vital moments in mind is when suddenly this sort of original or first thought *happens*, almost physically; and for that present duration there is no time or room yet for modesty or doubt or uncertainty. It feels just absolute; innocently, naively and excitedly absolute, at the point of occurrence, says James—as he expresses it in the first important paper he published:

> The Absolute is what has not yet been transcended, criticised or made relative. So far from being something quintessential and unattainable as is so often pretended, it is practically the most familiar thing in life. Every thought is absolute to us at the moment of conceiving it or acting upon it. It only becomes relative in the light of further reflection.[3]

It only 'becomes' relative when we have to go back into the world of further connections, sensible qualifications, mundane reservations, and firm boundaries again. But then imagine the first time this very shift from absolute to relative occurred, psychologically. For humans nothing has the original force of the relative, save through the experience of something first felt as lone and absolute, that then has to undergo the (often painful) process of correction and adjustment. Otherwise relativism is just the secondary, play-it-safe, pre-emptive apology of 'That is just my view...' The initial absolutism and the individualism that goes with it will always be checked in good time by both other people and other considerations; but it is the unchecked and unapologetic and un-self-conscious first impulse that creates the initial disruptive opening in reality. 'Every thought is absolute to us at the moment of conceiving it or acting upon it.'

The best living moments, James concludes, 'have somewhat of [the] absolute that needs no lateral support. Their meaning seems to well up from out of their very centre, in a way impossible verbally to describe', and as in joy they are sudden glimpses of a wonderful 'little absolute'.[4] It is like a small feeling of genius.

What is going on here? The Plough, the renewal of thoughts about Time and Space, the strange relation of personality and matter, the momentary absolute and its turn into the relative. These are some of James's stranger thoughts about the coming-into-being of our reality. If I cannot explain exactly *how* one made me think of another, nonetheless the connecting, as James put it, '*is* the thinking'.[5] For the inside experience of these large odd thoughts, and their implicit connection, does not feel simply abstract, intellectual, or impersonal. To me they feel, as James says, rather amazingly 'familiar', as if they were deep-level clues. Clues, that is to say, to the mental potential underlying our selves and our lives which we may individually may tap into. They seem to begin to offer some sort of autobiographical use.

To take up just one now: that thing about the absolute and the relative. Here is a more specific and embodied example from a novel by Stanley Middleton, concerning a retired educationalist, a lonely widower.

The man is reading C. S. Lewis's startling poem 'about Simon Magus finding Helen of Troy a housewife in Antioch and restoring her lost memory'. That sense of great change had transported him into a zone beyond his so that he had felt as he'd felt now and then as a schoolboy, on the brink of some novelty beyond the temporal, near some life-lifting, -shifting strait of discovery. He had been too clever, crafty, cautious or worldly as a grown man at his work; the minor brilliances, glimpses into the ineffable, had been, properly, lost.

He couldn't quite define what it was that so thrilled him, and then it disappeared, as if only what was immediately practical or obviously appropriate could be maintained. 'Excited, he jumped to his feet, made to the window with a young man's stride, and there he discovered old age again as he rested his forehead on the cold glass.'[6] Helen of Troy become common housewife, unconscious of her own mythic past—and the aged reader was momentarily a young superman again, on the verge of original discovery, before returning once more to the mundane and realistic.

Transport into a zone beyond his; some life-lifting or lift-shifting strait of discovery, with movement up and down as well as along; the brink of, minor brilliant glimpses into, the ineffable. The language here, even in the dismaying discovery of old age again, means such shifts are never automatic or negligible, though we may be used to thinking of them only as moods. But they are more than that, they are realizations that can move our very centres of gravity. There are times I have felt like that man in his second movement, the schoolboy re-discovering old age with surprised consternation, an excitement finding nothing to be done with it after all. But one of the best things I know—and know now all the more via William James—is that thoughts when they happen to you are never old. They renew. I don't mind so much about the returning to so-called normal afterwards, if one's very life has shifted, albeit temporarily.

More than just different 'points of view', really these are sudden emergent changes in the very topography of a person's being. James knew that topography, and the different confluent movements within it. He knew that the so-called self could expand or contract with knowledge and with emotion, and would fluctuate psychologically between revelation and disappointment, doubt and confidence—even between felt past and possible future—depending on its setting. And now I think I can say: this chapter is about that psychological topography, and James's sense of the dense and changing morphology of what he called mental fields.

*

It is important at this point to recall James's sense of the neurology underlying our mental set-up, that I tried initially to sketch out in Chapter 1.

Firstly, it isn't the case of there being simply two realms: mind within and world without. For James there were three departments of mind, each independent and yet co-operative.

One contains the sensory reception of the forces of foreign stimuli coming at you from all the force of life outside.

Then second, within the central nervous system there is a site for tense hesitation, a holding-place of preparation that results in the selection of a weighed response rather than an automatic reflex.

And this inner modification is given room just before, thirdly, there must be a discharged re-action back out into the world again, in behaviour and deed. 'The current of life which runs in at our ears and eyes is meant to run out at our hands, feet, or lips' ('Reflex Action and Theism'). Everything is finally geared towards that third department, out again.

So, department number two, as James calls it, is only a temporary medium. It hardly exists in its own right, except for being visualized as something sealed and hidden within the bony box that protects the brain. But it is where the origin of conscious *thinking* is: to transform a world made from incoming sensations into the somewhat different world that emerges through acts and ends and goals in response. This is thinking not so much in terms of explicit ideas but as a growing subjective centre in the midst and transition of things, from which you can begin reflexively to think of yourself as a thinker. And then as a thinker do something more with the pulses that pass through you. This middle department lives then 'between two fires' that never give it rest ('Reflex Action and Theism')—and that is why in that tension James will often look for any therapeutic aid that offers the respite of temporary relaxation, even regulated breathing.

Department two evolves as human beings no longer react as simply and automatically as animals can. And it keeps on developing till the nervous system becomes overloaded, and consciousness comes into being 'for the sake of steering a nervous system grown too complex to regulate itself' (*PP* 1, p. 144, chapter 5, 'Automaton Theory'). The conscious mind can hesitate, can intervene in its own processes, can work back and forth between passive and active, between finding and making. We have to learn that we possess it and can use it.

But then James adds a further layer of consideration: for all its development, our nervous system still remains of limited capacity, with finite supplies of energy. So if it has become too complex to regulate itself automatically, and has to employ consciousness in self-regulation, involving as that does the demand of extra power, then it has in turn to conserve some of its limited energy-supply, to make savings somewhere, in order not to break down. That conservation takes place by relegating as much activity as possible back down again to a level of new human automaticity that we call unthinking habit and common routine, thereby freeing up consciousness to use the left-over energy for the crucial and exceptional work of attention, choice and will. As a neurophysiologist James could see that this had indeed happened, that only a small part of neural activity was concerned with consciousness, and that a large part of cognitive activity needed not to be conscious at all.

This economy was necessary to enable consciousness, but it also demanded further trade-offs within the field of consciousness itself. In 'What Psychical Research Has Accomplished', James described how his fellow psychologist F. W. H. Myers had likened ordinary consciousness to the visible part of the spectrum of light. Invisibly beyond it there was the psychological and psychic equivalent to ultra-violet rays and infra-red energy. During the long evolution of human beings, there had been a continual displacement of the threshold—the 'limen'—of consciousness. Natural selection had raised certain faculties above that threshold whenever they were found especially necessary for survival: they became 'supra-liminal', part of the agenda and apparatus for the conscious continuance of normal life, till eventually they could become automatic again. But other ultra-violet or infra-red powers, not called into consciousness as immediately useful, were stored 'subliminally' in unconscious memory. There they waited, latent and potential, for the need and the call, and the release of sufficient energy to enable their emergence.

Mainly we can live on auto-pilot. It is only under the pressure of extraordinary circumstances—above all for James in moments of personal and spiritual crisis—that our capacity for extra individual power, for some creative freedom to choose amongst alternatives, is most fully released. Even so, small versions of the extraordinary occur regularly, and the occurrence of the extraordinary remains always potential.

James relished the pressures that created our psychological economy. Only a small proportion of the bombardment of information processed at any moment can be contained within a single stable focus. Only a limited amount of human capability can be harnessed on any one occasion. We can only take so much, and we can only deploy so much. The rest has to be fuzzily peripheral, and left implicit in the surrounding background, or stored below the level of consciousness. And so much has to remain peripheral or sunken, until the focus alters to take in a changed point of view, to allow and respond to a new emergent realization. 'Consciousness has a two-part structure: a focussed region of articulated experience surrounded by a field of relatively unarticulated vague experience.' The focus James calls the 'nucleus'; the surrounds are best understood as a 'fringe', with a sense there of 'a more'.[7] James's field theory derived from Faraday's work on electro-magnetic forces, a world made not so much of solid matter as fields of energy. But in James, the physics became psychological and existential.

Typically, James would turn to his lecture audience to explain this structural economy, on the spot, in simple practical terms:

> You, for example, now, although you are also thinking and feeling, are getting through your eyes sensations of my face and figure, and through your ears sensations of my voice.
>
> (*Talks*, chapter 2, 'The Stream of Consciousness')

Those sensations are probably at this moment the primary centre or focus or nucleus of your present conscious field; the thoughts and feelings are at the periphery, margin, or fringe.

> On the other hand, some object of thought, some distant image, may have become the focus of your mental attention even whilst I am speaking…and in that case, the sensations of my face and voice, although not absolutely vanishing from your conscious field, may have taken up a very faint and marginal place.   (*Talks*, chapter 2)

James took the idea of a field of vision and turned it into a field of consciousness, and that field exists not only inside the mind but opening out into the world, in its sense of space and its experience of time. The temporal dimension means that the field of consciousness is in almost continual mutation around a relatively stable nucleus: now I am looking at the lecturer, now I am thinking more of what he is saying, now I am thinking of something else. Mostly the changes are minor and unnoticed, but sometimes they become sufficient to affect and shift the centre, altering the very composition of the force-field.

James would then turn to his audience in the lecture room, this time from his own point of view, typically taking a micro example from the fringes of grammar and applying it live:

> The word 'or' names a genuine reality. Thus, as I speak here, I may look ahead, *or* to the right *or* to the left.
>
> (*A Pluralistic Universe*, 'Conclusions')

And it is not even that there are simply three separate alternative spots—now right, now left, now centre—that can act as the focus. Rather, the intervening space between them gives the lecturer a momentary intimation in transit—a 'virtual' sense otherwise impossible—of the whole field of possible points of view.

He knows the room is full. Through the mind's eye this is a way of seeing what you don't quite see, or cannot see all at once, but can only infer in transition. Yet the virtual is there always; it is not merely a possible: 'The difference between virtuality and barely abstract possibility is thus this,' writes James, 'that the former is *grounded* while the latter floats in our mind loosely with no associates in fact'(MEN p. 36)[8] The virtual is grounded because the conditions that would make it *appear* are already there, like all the seating in the lecture theatre, like all the words that could be used when you are searching for the right one. And appearance here is not something *opposed* to reality: appearance is a greater or lesser manifestation of reality on any single occasion: that is the sort of radical re-description in James that opens up a field of inquiry. So in a state of depression, for example, there is no looking to right or left for alternatives, nothing good appears possible, and the virtual is almost kept out, like a thought denied and suppressed and never given room.

James loved varying his terms—focus and margin; substantive and transitive; centre and periphery; nucleus and fringe, fringe or aura or halo or penumbra: he loved language when it reappeared anew in different circumstances over the years of his writing life, not statically applied and re-applied as labels, but changing as dynamically as what it described. So we cannot look to him for consistent definitions of 'the virtual' as compared to 'the possible' or 'the potential' or 'the implicit' – all are on the fringes of consciousness, in the background to the perception of reality and part of its meaning. But for the most part it goes something like this with him, in terms of the distinctions. The *virtual* is always real, as the stars are, as the different sides of the lecture room are, though not always and never fully actualized. *Potential* is more like a single version of the virtual, feeding forward, immanent, indeterminate, and unknown until bursting into actualization, into living proof, within individual practice. And *possibility* is what is more generally established after a potential has been successfully actualized in a particular case: possibilities form the definite palette of *implicit* feasibilities known in advance, floatingly available, and sometimes made explicitly manifest. But above all:

> The important fact which this 'field' formula commemorates is the indetermination of the margin. Inattentively realized as is the matter which the margin contains, it is nevertheless there, and helps both to guide our behaviour and to determine the next movement of our attention. It lies around us like a 'magnetic field', inside of which our centre of energy turns like a compass-needle, as the present phase of consciousness enters into its successor. Our whole past store of memories floats beyond this margin, ready at a touch to come in; and the entire mass of residual powers, impulses, and knowledges that constitute our empirical self stretches continuously beyond it. So vaguely drawn are the outlines between what is actual and what is only potential at any moment of our conscious life, that it is always hard to say of certain mental elements whether we are conscious of them or not.
>
> (VRE, p. 182, lecture 10, 'Conversion')

That is the supreme importance of the field: it obliterates the simple once-and-for all-distinction between actual and potential; they are to be decided again and again within the field and its own changes. 'The process by which one dissolves into another is often very gradual, and all sorts of inner rearrangements of contents occur. Sometimes the focus remains but little changed, whilst the margin alters rapidly. Sometimes the focus alters, and the margin stays. Sometimes focus and margin change places. Sometimes, again, abrupt alterations of the whole field occur' (*Talks*, chapter 2).

Some fields are evanescent like mental weather, and others more stable and well-bounded. Some are wide and vibrant, offering at their faintest margins glimpses 'of what we seem rather to be about to perceive rather than to perceive actually'; while others become so narrow-minded and so literal-minded, in times of illness and fatigue for example, that 'we find ourselves oppressed and contacted' (*VRE*, p. 181, lecture 10, 'Conversion'). For some human beings the movement from one context to another is only an adjustment within their existing field, while in others it causes a radically 'discordant splitting' (*PP* 1, p. 294, chapter 10, 'The Consciousness of Self').

A simple example of this fluid movement would be the way that James sees adjectives as often ambiguous or wandering 'as if uncertain where to fix themselves'. We can talk of the experience of painful objects or we can speak instead of painful experiences, of feelings of anger or angry feelings, wicked desires or desires for wickedness, seductive visions or visions of seductive things: qualities rest ambiguously between the physical and the mental, in the mind and in the thing (*Essays in Radical Empiricism*, 1912, 'Does Consciousness Exist?'). Such movements speak of something that is more like osmosis than the bounded separation of inner and outer worlds. And in this fluctuation, the same object can take up different positions. My body is sometimes me, but sometimes only a part of what I am; my children may be as dear to me as my body is and arouse the same feelings if attacked, and yet can also be quite separate (*PP* 1, p. 291, chapter 10, 'The Consciousness of Self'). So, emotional states such as happiness or depression are fields and what is more, fields that at certain times for certain people can seem completely separate from each other, even mutually exclusive, as if they were indeed absolute:

Happiness, like every other emotional state, has blindness and insensibility to opposing facts given it as its instinctive weapon for self-protection against disturbance. When happiness is actually in possession, the thought of evil can no more acquire the feeling of reality than the thought of good can gain reality when melancholy rules.

(VRE p. 74, lecture 4, 'The Religion of Healthy-Mindedness')

'If we be joyous, we cannot keep thinking of those uncertainties and risks which abound upon our path; if lugubrious, we cannot think of new triumphs, travels, loves and joys' (PP 2, p. 563, chapter 26, 'Will'). Happiness or melancholy: either way they become for their duration psychological worlds of their own, more or less lasting. As centres or nuclei, they are like people trying to survive, taking over the very persons who are their host, trying to sustain belief in their world alone. And yet other worlds and other views and other feelings exist virtually, at the same time. There may be initially no more than a slight alteration in attention: so normal, so natural, that we are hardly surprised by it. But the shorthand name for any candidate for greater attention may be something like the feeling of 'or'—a non-sensory figure that enters consciousness by making fewer demands on its energy than the host of past and possible sensory experiences it cognitively represents.[9] Anything a little more inconsistent or surprising than usual may begin the process of shift:

A mental system may be undermined or weakened by this interstitial alteration just as a building is, and yet for a time keep upright by dead habit. But a new perception, a sudden emotional shock...

(VRE, p. 156, lecture 9, 'Conversion')

'Interstitial' is brilliant: we hardly see in the midst of apparently larger things all that is coming through tiny microscopic cracks, registering the effect if at all only out of the corner of our eyes or at the back of our mind. And yet it has its marginal effect, sub-consciously and cumulatively, until at some crucial tipping-point the centre of consciousness *is* affected, and some aspect of life (an experience, a fact, an idea) that was left outside consciousness, or on its periphery, begins to intensify and take over. This becomes a system changed by what is admitted into it, by its own content eventually boiling over and re-forming itself. Our best is found when we inhabit the richest, most mobile field that we can, the most emotional, the most potentially meaningful, and not the most easily captured or narrowly defined. 'A degree of vagueness is what best consists with fertility' (PP 1, p. 6, chapter 1, 'The Scope of Psychology'). 'This very vagueness' of a nervous system not fully stable, at work in a field of endeavour at once not too ordered or too chaotic, consti-tutes an advantage—allowing its 'possessor to adapt his conduct to the minutest alterations in the environing circumstances' (PP 1, p. 139, chapter 5, 'The Automaton Theory'). It is why some people like me believe they think best within the realm of literature.

This still feels like a new way of being. It means that for James the self, and its consciousness, is not a separate, isolated substance but is a vibrating field opening out into the surrounding world. Moreover, what is vital is that the fringe does not merely surround the nucleus but permeates it with a fuller feeling of relation and meaning. The movements are liquid, with complicated cross-currents between conscious and non-conscious processing. Between the two, it was at the point of Myers's limen that James most wanted his thinking and his very self to exist, the creative point at which fields might change. Perhaps nothing was so won-derful to him as crossing a threshold, from one mental dimension into another, and carrying himself well through the crossing. To him, the movement of this sensitive organism from sub-conscious to conscious, from fringe to nucleus, was thought itself at its very best. The nucleus, the larger-scale substantively named centre, was in many ways the least important part of the whole thought-process.

What is important here is the idea of a continuous spectrum, as from 0 to 100—a range of constantly ongoing alterations from a merely momentary and passing shift of attention, to a temporary switch of a point of view, to a more permanent macro-experience of conversion. But the magnificent thing is that, throughout those varied alterations, the psychological process is the same, altering only in intensity of degree—as though clues to large things might come from very small versions of them. To say that a person is 'converted' (to anything) is testimony not to some extraordinary miracle separated by a chasm from other kinds of human life, but to a particularly powerful version of how ideas that were previously peripheral now take a central emotional place in the field of consciousness and, unlike passing thoughts or uneasy hesitations, consolidate into a new mental configuration. 'No chasm' exists between these different orders of experience: 'here, as elsewhere, nature shows continuous differences' and these differences are only 'matters of degree' (VRE, p. 187, lecture 10, 'Conversion').

In this dynamic rather than static world of meaning, even the admission of a single word and its surrounding vibration could affect the field:

> We have a thought, or we perform an act, repeatedly, but on a certain day the real meaning of the thought peals through us for the first time, or the act has suddenly turned into a moral impossibility. All we know is that there are dead feelings, dead ideas, and cold

beliefs, and there are hot and live ones; and when one grows hot and alive within us, everything has to re-crystallize about it.

(*VRE*, p. 155, lecture 9, 'Conversion')

This is an aesthetic sense of experience—not in the sense of being concerned solely with art or beauty as such, but because it is, as I argued in Chapter 2, agnostic and intuitive as to principles of selection and orientation. This was why James used the Faraday-derived analogy of 'a magnetic field, inside of which our centre of energy turns like a compass-needle' (*VRE*, p. 182, lecture 10, 'Conversion'). Directions are taken and choices made not out of deliberately religious or moral categorization but at risk or in venture, like an artist's or poet's instinctive warm seeking of what amidst the fields of life was most needed and best fitted, was nearest to what in the last chapter was called, after Bion, 'o'. That is the background power of the field: within it you can get signals from the virtual and the potential, from all that is not quite there and yet not non-existent, for orientation in this world.

What is more, the whole world of concrete objects and specific experiences is soaked through by abstractions and relations such as time and space but also by ideas such as goodness, beauty, and justice: 'We can never look directly at them, for they are bodiless and featureless and footless, but we grasp all other things by their means' (*VRE*, p. 50, lecture 3, 'The Reality of the Unseen'). That is one of the most important sentences James ever wrote. All the enabling background-experience that is implicit within the fringe, as tacit memory and feeling and relation, serves to provide intuitions for the centre by the signalling of neural messages. Through these antennae, in these messages, by a sort of radar, 'the most important element is…the mere feeling of harmony or discord, of a right or a wrong direction in the thought' (*PP* 1, p. 261, chapter 9,

'The Stream of Thought'). So: 'This' is hotter and more alive, it attracts us and fits with us; but 'That' feels colder and more dead, outside the current direction of our way. A suddenly increased intensity of feeling creates the thermal difference, disrupting linear processes, and making the field morph around it. We try, we should, to keep it alive.

For a thought has a life, a personal feel about it that is always more than we can ever explicitly define. And an individual is also like this: such that in the necessary economy required for consciousness, the shifting centre we call the self has all around it the aura of latent thoughts, memories, and abilities, shaken down into more than can ever be held consciously in mind together at any one moment. But all that implicit stuff is there, in the being of the person, ready to come forth, explicit, into mind or action when the need calls.

> I am aware of a constant play of furtherances and hindrances in my thinking, of checks and releases, tendencies which run with desire, and tendencies which run the other way…welcoming or opposing, appropriating or disowning, striving with or against, saying yes or no. This palpitating inward life is, in me, that central nucleus…
> (PP 1, p. 299, chapter 10, 'The Consciousness of Self')

A person is that palpitating field, and it makes a difference when he or she thinks in that way, instead of shrinking into a rigid, defensive, little core.

*

What is it actually like to have that living sense of a surrounding field? It is the personal that matters to William James, in having the first sense of reality. 'Individuality is founded in feeling; and the recesses of feeling, the darker, blinder strata of character, are the only places in the world in which we catch the real fact in the making, and directly perceive how events happen, and how work is actually done' (*VRE*, p. 380, lecture 20, 'Conclusions').

In the past, the great individuals were those who created a ferment in the world, utterly changing the field of endeavour. That is why William James relished the thought of Martin Luther as a 'religious genius' (*VRE*, p.14). Not for James's Luther was there to be merely institutional religion, organized through the intermediary forms of churches and priests and sacraments: 'It would profit us little to study this second-hand religious life. We must make search rather for the original experiences which were the pattern-setters' (*VRE*, p. 14, lecture 1 'Religion and Neurology'). It is then 'I, this individual I, just as I stand, without one plea' (*VRE*, p. 192, lecture 10, 'Conversion'). To James, Luther was like a renewal of the ferment of primitive Christianity. Christ, wrote Luther, 'died *not* to justify the righteous, but the *un*-righteous, and to make *them* the children of God' (*VRE*, p. 192, lecture 10 'Conversion'). In one great sentence, the shift of central nucleus from 'not the righteous' to 'the un-righteous' was a sort of conversion of the world, taking in all the weak and wretched impulses that the old pride of paganism had scorned. To win salvation, there could be no system of moral accountancy, the childish plus and minus of a righteous deed here, a guilty sin there and confessional afterwards; every little human make-do was taken away in the face of the Absolute. This was Luther 'sweeping off by a stroke of his hand the very notion of a debit and credit account kept with individuals by the Almighty'. He was 'rescuing theology from puerility' in 'the largeness of his conception of God' (*VRE*, p. 192, lecture 10 'Conversion'; p. 268, lecture 14, 'The Value of Saintliness').

It did not matter to his valuation that James did not believe as Luther had done. It did not matter if what had seemed so single-mindedly absolute to the unyielding Luther became relative in the course of history and subsequent thinking:

> Ptolemaic astronomy, euclidean space, aristotelian logic, scholastic metaphysics, were expedient for centuries, but human experience has boiled over those limits, we now call these things only relatively true, or true within those borders of experience.
>
> (*Pragmatism*, lecture 6 'Pragmatism's Conception of Truth')

Luther had changed a world-view, had created what Thomas Kuhn in *The Structure of Scientific Revolution*, first published in 1962, was to call a great paradigm shift, a seismic reformation, and revolution. Something of the absolute had burst into the relative, utterly transforming the field, breaking through mental containers, even as the wildness of genius erupts amidst the tame and mediocre.

But compared to Luther, James described himself as a religious *non*-genius, less a believer than a believer in believing—an agnostic to whom, at best, God was 'dimly real; not as an earthly friend'. James had only one very firm 'conviction', that '"normal" or "sane" consciousness is so small part of actual experience' and the nature of actual experience is something we have not been told the truth about.[10] With that he almost felt he could launch a new *psychological* reformation. 'As for me, my bed is made', he wrote the artist Sarah Whitman, 7 June 1899:

> I am against bigness and greatness in all their forms, and with the invisible molecular forces that work from individual to individual, stealing in through the crannies of the world like so many soft root-lets, or like the capillary oozing of water, and yet rending the hardest monuments of man's pride, if you give them time. The bigger the unit you deal with, the hollower, the more brutal, the more

mendacious is the life displayed. So I am against all big organizations as such, national ones first and foremost: against all big successes and big results; and in favor of the eternal forces of truth which always work in the individual and immediately unsuccessful way, under-dogs always, till history comes after they are long dead, and puts them on the top.—You need take no notice of these ebullitions of spleen, which are probably quite unintelligible to any one but myself.[11]

The immediate context for this avowal were problems with expansion at Harvard, and more widely, with expansionism in America's imperialistic foreign policy in the Philippines. Organizations and countries alike became rigidly institutionalized by forgetting their originating impulses even in the effort to establish themselves more and more powerfully. It was only in relationships of talking and listening and imagining, in the inner workings of teaching and writing and reading, that subliminal forces were vitally communicated between one individual and another. And so in all this, James knew he had not the bigness and the greatness of a Luther. He knew that he could not offer what Luther gave, an actual substance, so to speak, to rest upon; a definitive and holy faith. In a modern world increasingly without the religious tradition which those such as Luther had created and re-created, human beings were driven, teleological creatures that now had no clear end for that drive. What James had to offer was not a great end like Luther, or like Bunyan's in the Heavenly City, but more a method and a sense of life by which to work, in small, within the crannies of the world.

The key to that method lay in his last essay 'The Moral Equivalent to War'. There again it was not the old aggressions or the great fights that any longer pertained to James, but their transformation into smaller, subtler modern forms. In the field of any modern controversy, said James, thinkers from now on should always take on the shock of entering the point of view of their opponents and really feeling its life. This was not just a matter of liberal tolerance: such tolerance, however benign or salutary a habit, was not the living thought that shakes and unsettles. What James was urging was more to do with the dynamism of getting their thoughts into your mind, and seeing what you could do with them, and what they did with you, deep down inside there. First truly enter the point of view. But then in the second place, says James quoting just four crucial words from his friend, John Jay Chapman, 'Then move the point' ('The Moral Equivalent of War'). Move the point is what shifts the field.

The pragmatic question is always finally this: what does this mean as applied to real life? what actual difference does it make to 'move the point'? It is as James the teacher put it in relation to education at the end of his *Talks to Teachers on Psychology*:

> Spinoza long ago wrote in his *Ethics* that anything that a man can avoid under the notion that it is bad he may also avoid under the notion that something else is good. He who habitually acts...under the negative notion, the notion of the bad, is called a slave by Spinoza. To him who acts habitually under the notion of good he gives the name of freeman. See to it now, I beg you, that you make freemen of your pupils by habituating them to act, whenever possible, under the notion of a good.   (*Talks*, chapter 15, 'The Will')

Move the point from fearing the bad to wanting the good. Squeeze the slave out of yourself. To be free is a subtle shift, a use of mental department two to employ what James was the first to call 'plasticity' (PP 1, p. 105, chapter 4, 'Habit')—which here meant creatively turning one thing into another, better version of itself. For 'the great thing in all education is to make our nervous system'—and above all its tendency to form habits—'our ally instead of our enemy' (*Talks*, chapter 8, 'The Laws of Habit'). What begins as our friend—the need to economize on what has to be conscious—becomes our foe when habit turns into a taking for granted. But our enemy becomes our friend again when we can help consolidate good things into new habits *and* still keep revising them.

Find out the point of view, the central intensity of interest, from which your pupils start; then move the point, says James to the teachers of future generations. Put the same thing into a different place, help give it a different orientation, and stabilize its altered field:

> Respect then, I beg you, always the original reactions, even when you are seeking to overcome their connection with certain objects, and to supplant them with others that you wish to make the rule. Bad behavior, from the point of view of the teacher's art, is as good a starting-point as good behavior. In fact, paradoxical as it may sound to say so, it is often a better starting-point than good behavior would be.
>
> (*Talks*, chapter 7, 'What the Native Reactions Are')

'The wretch languishing in the felon's cell may be drinking draughts of the wine of truth that will never pass the lips of the so-called favorite of fortune' ('The Dilemma of Determinism').

So spoke James the dissident, the man who knew the secret paradoxes that could hardly be spoken without fear of hubris, and yet are there. Misery, difficulty, unruliness and crisis could—for some people at least—be the best allies; wrong things were right things out of place; what could come from small shifts and re-workings in the search for the right place were wonderful surprises and unsuspected powers. This was what could happen within the field if one could keep it relatively undamaged, let it make repairs, make it work.

'I do not seek, I find' was Picasso's watchword for creative bravery. In fact, what James shows is how the seeking often goes on sub-consciously, in tacit alert, within the finding. One model for such a venture was the poet whom James himself most read for succour in his youthful depression. In *The Excursion* and *The Prelude*, Wordsworth used his antennae to sense when his life was on track, when his feelings were on the right wavelength, when whatever he had inchoately behind and beneath him was finding some fit in what was outside and ahead. Not in Cambridge, not in London, not in the failure of the vision of the French Revolution. 'A feeling that I was not for that hour/Not for that place' (*The Prelude*, 1850, 3.81–2). But home in Grasmere, in a larger sense of the universe lodged within one small part of it. It was an epic achievement to feel so seriously the inner obligation of one's own life, and significantly it was made by a poet in the effort to stay in touch with his poetic powers, through a dark workmanship not limited to his own control. As Wordsworth walked his native lands, on return from the places where he had not prospered, his rural neighbours 'must have thought him a very insignificant and foolish personage,' wrote James, 'It surely never occurred to any one of them to wonder what was going on inside of *him* or what it might be worth' ('On a Certain Blindness in Human Beings').

But this is not solely about being a poet, a Wordsworth or a Frost. James's most central fear is, as in depression, that what's potential in a person cannot make its way out into any kind of existence. Action, almost any constructive action is the need: sometimes taking the form of vital thinking and feeling; sometimes writing, especially when that makes a difference to a reader; sometimes thoughts that affect one's own behaviour; sometimes a sense of personal service to the larger world. If emotions pass without prompting any deed, if responses to any experience remain only intellectual, not only is the occasion gone, but the effort-making capacity itself begins to wither. There is no point in being affected by what you read in a book or hear in a concert, says James emphatically, 'without expressing it afterward in *some* active way':

> Let the expression be the least thing in the world—speaking geni-ally to one's aunt, or giving up one's seat in a horse-car, if nothing more heroic offers—but let it not fail to take place.
>
> (PP 1, p. 126, chapter 4, 'Habit')

A struggling old man can no longer dig out the root of a rotten tree, a young passer-by does it for him at one stroke, with vigour's ease. But then the very gratefulness of the weak and tearful elder upsets him. The young man was Wordsworth in an ostensibly simple little poem 'Simon Lee', a poem and a poet unafraid of seeming merely mundane—'O Reader! had you in your mind/ Such stores as silent thought can bring':

> O gentle Reader! you would find
> A tale in every thing.

And so James: 'All Goods are disguised by the vulgarity of their concomitants, in this work-a-day world; but woe to him who can only recognise them...in their pure and abstract form' (PP 1 p. 125, chapter 4, 'Habit').

This book is about trying to use artistic thinking, and above all literary ways of thinking, in apparently non-artistic and non-literary settings. It is James Applied in this work-a-day world. Chapter 5 will be another attempt to see what it can and cannot do.

'WHAT DOES *NOT* WORK'— THOMAS HARDY

Into a notebook, on 21 August 1925, Thomas Hardy copied from a magazine article these words: '"Truth is what will work" said Wm. James'. He added drily: 'A worse corruption of language was never perpetrated.'[1] For Hardy, it needed to be put the other way. Truth is precisely what does *not* work. In so far as human beings experienced it, Truth was most often the reality that prevents or resists or ignores us. And even that was to anthropomorphize the sheer indifference of the non-human system.

To Hardy, humans and their whole cognitive apparatus for the finding of significance were an evolutionary accident. We had not only blindly evolved, wrote Hardy, we had *over*-evolved, cut loose beyond clear purpose:

> A woeful fact – that the human race is too extremely developed for its corporeal conditions, the nerves being evolved to an activity abnormal in such an environment. Even the higher animals are in excess in this respect. It may be questioned if Nature, or what we call Nature, so far back as when we crossed the line from invertebrates to vertebrates, did not exceed its mission. This planet does not supply the materials for happiness to higher existences. Other planets may, though one can hardly see how.   (7 April 1889)[2]

This for Hardy was the almost unspeakable paradox: that so-called 'Nature' had thoughtlessly evolved what Nature itself could not then satisfy—a human creature of gifts at once higher than, and yet still subjected to, the unthinking forces that made it. There was not even something that called itself Nature. There was no such noun, no language, no grammar in the non-human universe, no intention or meaning outside the human need for it. There was no one to blame; no God, and no basis or support for emotions like blame. 'The emotions have no place in a world of defect, and it is a cruel injustice that they have developed in it' (9 May 1881, *TH Life*, p. 153).

No, no, no. It is like switching worlds, even planets, to turn from Hardy back to James again. Hardy's over-evolution was in James's world human life overflowing its initial prompts. It is 'the excess of function that necessarily accompanies the working of every complex machine' until it is no longer a machine (*Talks to Teachers*, chapter 3, 'The Child as a Behaving Organism'). This evolved human nature was going on to demand its own new, secondary, brain-born ideals. And James is wholly agnostic—cannot for certain know, and at some level does not have to care yet—as to whether that hazardous human autonomy is in defiance of creation or part of its development. It is an even bet.

Too much is a good in James, where it is a pain in Hardy. That is what Marilynne Robinson, for one, admires in James, 'the feeling of an overplus of meaning in reality' that won't be contained for long even by our own formulae.[3] It is what both produces and results from James' astonishing sentences, the mind-spinning overplus of a sentence such as: 'Realities are not *true*, they *are*; and beliefs are true *of* them' (*The Meaning of Truth*, chapter 8, 'The Pragmatist Account of Truth'). There is something wonderful in that bare 'are'; something wonderful in the discovery of those realities *through* us, as being even so independent *of* us. The prepositions mark the precise complexity of the field.

But in this counter-chapter, I change the field with the entry of Hardy, to say: what if William James does not work? That after all was not a predicament, a threat, or a way of thinking, that James himself was ever secure from, in that underlying sadness which John Jay Chapman saw in him, always menacing. His life's work, suggested Chapman, was to have what he called 'a purgatorial influence', to get whomsoever he connected with *out* of hell on earth.[4] In this chapter, Hardy represents something of that hell on earth—the challenge that the poet Robert Frost, student of James, admirer of Hardy, acknowledges in a notebook: 'One good thing about Hardy. – He has planted himself on the wrongs that can't be righted.'[5]

*

But first, before confronting Thomas Hardy and what can't be righted, I want to turn back to the close of my previous chapter: to James on teaching and education, on the growth of small things, and the choices and futures of the young whom he influenced. I want to think about what James offers in practical terms of hopeful growth and possible development. And then I will let Hardy loose upon him.

James knew from his own experience that even for the young, the talented and the fortunate, possibilities could not be lived upon for ever. The day of decision must come and, all too often, some youth, even though rather privileged in education and upbringing, simply surrenders to taking a place in the commercial world, say, rather than something less certain and lucrative, and is then committed:

> Little by little, the habits, the knowledge, of the other career, which
> once lay so near, cease to be reckoned even among his possibilities.
> At first, he may sometimes doubt whether the self he murdered in
> that decisive hour might not have been the better of the two; but
> with the years such questions themselves expire, and the old alter-
> native ego, once so vivid, fades into something less substantial than
> a dream.   ('Great Men and Their Environment')

And so such lives narrow, habits predominate, and alternatives
are gradually but inexorably destroyed. As a student, James's best
friend at Harvard from 1864 was Oliver Wendell Holmes, two
young men fervently involved together in philosophical discussion. But in 1868 Holmes wrote James that he had finally decided
to give himself to the Law, to reconcile himself to life, as he put it,
for fear of utter formlessness. The best he could do was still, within
that chosen field, to try to maintain his ideals on the horizon as
'vanishing points', he wrote, to give a perspective, a steer, and a
direction.[6] The friendship more or less split at that point, as the
two parted course. James loved the image of the ideals remaining
as vanishing points on the horizon, and understood the imperative to give life a specific form and purpose. But it must have
seemed to him, struggling as he then was to resist a final commitment to medicine, that Holmes had deserted him. Holmes was to
become the great American jurist of his age. And he remained
true to Harvard's pragmatic principles: that the life of the law lay
not in strict logic but in the complexity of experience; that real-
world outcomes and consequences were vital. But between the
two of them, fairly or not, it must have seemed to James that
Holmes had gone closer to choosing Self than Soul: success,
career, effectiveness, and compromise. Self or Soul are the orientation points that Mark Edmundson, a latter-day reader of James,
offers as the essential choice in a life, albeit with all the individual

variations of shade and degree that lie across the spectrum. For James, Self was at best no more and no less than what it was for his beloved Walt Whitman: a way of toughing out his tenderness, to protect and defend a Soul that found a place for itself only really through writing.[7]

But still the voice of that writing tried to reach back out to the reader, that 'you be my poem', wrote Whitman. That the poem be turned into a life. Never to be moved by a book, a play, a concert, was James's mantra, 'without expressing it afterwards in *some* active way' (*PP* 1, p. 126, chapter 4, 'Habit'). So much depended on the difference actually made in the world, on how much could go into or was squeezed out of the practical outcomes of a life.

I do not 'derive benefit' from William James, says another reader; instead, better—less narrowly but more emotionally—'he does me good'.[8] But what good could James do? Did James work? Hardy said he didn't.

One crucial test-case is W. E. B. Du Bois, who, throughout a life committed to being practical *and* idealistic, considered himself a Jamesian pragmatist. In 1895 Du Bois was the first African American to obtain a doctorate from Harvard, on 'The suppression of the African slave trade in the United States, 1638–1871'. James had urged him as an undergraduate to use his philosophical understanding not as an academic spectator or abstract commentator but in application to specific historical and social problems. Accordingly Du Bois' thesis was work that fitted his life and background, and prepared him for future activism. The very thought of Du Bois added extra personal feeling to James's own opposition to the continuing horrors of lynching, alongside the work of John Jay Chapman in politics and Oliver Wendell Holmes in the law-courts.

But coming from a mixed-race heritage, Du Bois was most acutely aware of a sense of 'twoness': 'an American, a Negro; two souls, two thoughts'.[9] Exceptionally educated as he was, first through money raised by his neighbours, later through loans, inheritances, summer work and scholarships, Du Bois did not fit easily in either world. But he committed himself to holding that anomalous position in the middle of things. Within individuals, the conversion of painful subjective experience into an objective existence, an unremitting fact in the world, was the beginning of a moral assertion. William James had written of the psychology of the divided self. But all that Du Bois could do initially was to keep the twoness together, the tensions 'unreconciled', but contained 'in one dark body', 'whose dogged strength alone keeps it from being torn asunder' (*The Souls of Black Folk*, p. 3).

He 'would not Africanize America' since America had become a new home that had 'too much to teach the world', as he himself had learnt at Harvard. But equally he 'would not bleach his Negro soul in a flood of white Americanism' since he knew that 'Negro blood has a message for the world' (*The Souls of Black Folk*, pp. 3–4). We come not empty-handed, he wrote, not even in our poverty:

> the spiritual striving of the freedmen's sons is the travail of souls whose burden is almost beyond the measure of their strength, but who bear it in the name of an historic race, in the name of this the land of their fathers' fathers, and in the name of human opportunity.   (*The Souls of Black Folk*, p. 12)

We, says Du Bois, are the spirit of the Declaration of Independence, amidst the land of green dollar and smart fashion, in the simple beauty of our cry: 'The Music of Negro religion is that plaintive rhythmic melody, with its touching minor cadences, which despite caricature and defilement, still remains the most original and beautiful expression of human life and longing yet born on American soil' (*The Souls of Black Folk*, p. 191). There were daily examples of the gifts that his people had to offer. Black women offered mother-love to white children within their parents' homes, yet only to be treated as servants, if not slaves.

Double consciousness meant always having to look at yourself, shamed or diminished, through the eyes of the white majority, even whilst struggling to develop your own freed resources from within. This racial trauma, derived from slavery, is what even a hundred years on, the writer of *No Win Race* still describes, in his being what he poignantly calls 'a pre-emptive person'. That is: one who carries with him the old insecure and persecuted feeling, still deeply ingrained within the nervous system—'when I'd notice a policeman staring at me...when walking down a side road and seeing a group of white boys...when going into a shop with an item purchased in another store'. Get your response ready beforehand; think what might happen next.[10] That nervous pre-emption is exactly the opposite of what James and Du Bois wanted for people: precursive faith, prevenient courage, the confidence that defiantly in advance of evidence for success helps to create that success.

It was said, noted Du Bois, that the hesitant and fitful efforts of the journeyman black craftsman were proof of the race's inherent inferiority and weakness. But it was the other way round, he insisted: the potential strength and the confidence to bring that strength into effect were continually being sapped by the white community's disparagement. Always William James thinks of what human beings can add to the world. But the mathematics here work differently: it is through 'the contradiction of double aims', American and African, that the artisan 'had but *half a heart in either cause*':

> This waste of double aims, this seeking to satisfy two unreconciled ideals, has wrought sad havoc with the courage and faith and deeds of ten thousand thousand people...and *at times has even seemed about to make them ashamed of themselves.* (*The Souls of Black Folk*, pp. 4–5)

'*About* to' was in its James-like language the last small opening for an alternative future route, before shame contracted the whole field of possibility. Still Du Bois fought for education there, and not just skills. For him, unlike other more narrowly practical reformers such as Booker T. Washington,[11] education was not just the acquisition of the technological abilities so that black artisans might climb higher on the American economic ladder. It was also to create the inner resources for a moral stand within the nation. It was the means to make and to sustain a life from within, the inner force of a culture, a history, and a vocation, whatever might be happening in the life outside. The *Souls* of Black Folk.

But what split and damaged the United States was 'the problem of the color-line' in the boundaries and clefts it created across the whole human field (*The Souls of Black Folk*, p. 40). In chapter 2 of *The Souls of Black Folk*, Du Bois turns from stereotypes to thinks of two particular individuals, two old Southerners broken in the chaotic aftermath of the civil war. One is an aged black woman, freed too late, all her sons, by the white slave master whose own family she also tended, left murdered by vigilantes. The other, an old white man who had only reluctantly gone along with slavery, his sons buried in nameless graves as a result of the country's war, leaving him now filled with more hate towards the North and the blacks than he had ever felt before. Both these people are 'incongruous elements left arrayed against each other' (p. 29), where 'incongruous' is just the word William James himself might have chosen in the face of reductive categories. They are equally 'two passing figures of the present-past', writes Du Bois (p. 30), who are left suffering in the most similar ways from recent history; while no one—especially not he—was able to join their hands together across the continuing divide. That was the failure of what should have been (in James's terms) a communal 'partaking' in the republic. For Du Bois the rebuilding of that republic had to go back to the failure of Reconstruction during the 1860s and 1870s, the period following the civil war and after the death of Abraham Lincoln, when newly freed slaves in the South failed to receive true freedom. A second Reconstruction was necessary to retrieve the broken principles of the failed first, to recover the stuff of lost potential, and rescuing the alternative story from its oblivion, give it a new route. It was to be a wonderful re-shaping of time: a present that had betrayed what should have been its past heritage, was to rescue the beliefs, hopes, and plans of that lost past in order to make again a worthy future.

But Du Bois was never a cannily professional politician. He worked from 'a certain tingling challenge of risk', and often finding himself out of step with his allies as well as his opponents, was always struggling to find the right political tactic at the right time.[12] Black America is travelling, he wrote, a curious path that 'turns and twists so frequently that one cannot see just where one is going'.[13] What he got from James was all that James ever claimed to offer: an instigation, a sense of potential in the past and in the future, and a way of orientation.

As it was, in the distortion of a nation's moral vision, the souls and not just the selves of African Americans were banished, unthought of, to the fringes of society, to the realm of outcasts from the focal norm. That is how Jamesian psychology provided the basis for Du Bois' social politics. It was a philosophical psychology that helped develop 'the habit of always seeing an alternative, of not taking the usual for granted, of making conventionalities fluid again, of imagining foreign states of mind' ('The Teaching of Philosophy in Our Colleges'). Human varieties, like the varieties of religious experience, were to be genuinely met and celebrated, partaken of as changes that could also change those who gladly encountered them. Of other things, of other peoples, James wrote exuberantly: 'Is not my knowing them at all a gift and not a right?...*Data! gifts!* something to be thankful for! It is a gift that we can approach things at all, and by means of the time and space of which our minds and they partake, alter our actions so as to meet them' ('On Some Hegelisms'). To re-create such a world in which encounter and consciousness itself might feel like small but wonderful revelations, Du Bois's people needed, it seemed to James, an equivalent Martin Luther to force an opening of closed minds, to revolutionize the field and shift the colour line. For James it would always have to be a *person* who would dramatically embody the idea and individually represent the pent-up force. It had to be personal: it disappointed James that he himself was not sufficiently a believer as to experience God personally, as a felt presence, to whom one could pray.

In the spirit of his Harvard education, Du Bois had duly begun as a reforming liberal, believing that prejudice was the result of an ignorance and ill-will that could be overcome through the raised consciousness resulting from education, from civil rights, and from closer co-existence. But increasingly in the face of long years of continuing resistance, Du Bois came to see prejudice as something that in its unreachable tenacity conscious education could not wholly reach. It was formed of deep *unconscious* habit. James had been the first to describe the power of such habit, and Du Bois went on to read Freud too on the power of the unconscious. But beyond the psychologists, he also found Karl Marx. The ugly habit of racial prejudice was created not just by uneducated psychological ignorance but by the undisclosed power of long-embedded economic interests. Through Marx, Du Bois came to see that this deeply intractable unconsciousness was the result of the white mind-set defending for its very life an ideology of 'property'. That ideology simply could not admit the idea of natural gifts or unpaid generosity, and survive.

The force of that deep structural resistance left Du Bois at the end of his life a ninety-year-old exile, trying to make a home in Ghana, in place of an America that had rejected him. Du Bois had been brought to trial in 1951, in the McCarthyite era, accused of being a 'foreign agent' because of his Marxist socialism and interest in the Russian Revolution. Though not convicted, it left him internally damaged, and externally shunned even by reformist organizations on his own side, fearing to be associated with him. By the time of his death in 1963, aged ninety-five, he was planning and editing a multi-volume *Encyclopedia Africana* as part of the growing Pan-African movement, recovering its lost history. But even that was left unfinished at his death and, with dwindling financial support, was never completed in the form he envisioned, as a great bringing together of the African diaspora in volumes that would stand as the new African heritage.

The field Du Bois had chosen, with the uncertain time-scale of political achievement, had always left him at the mercy of what could or could not be achieved in the world. For all his awareness that the project was too great *not* to be fallible and beyond immediate resolution, Du Bois could not help the bitter feeling that his United States mission had failed. He felt the lack of recognition, the rejection and humiliation there. His definition of a deep social problem was: the failure of a social group, for reasons internal and external, to be able to find and realize its own needs and ideals, and adapt a desired line of action to the given conditions of the time. In the face of that deep problem and its personal consequences for himself, he was bound to ask himself how much his move to Nigeria and Ghana was a fundamental recovery of his project, or a banishment and refuge. In his final fragmentary *Autobiography* collected and edited by his literary executor and published posthumously in 1968, he insisted that he still embodied the thwarted needs of his people. Even now at the point of his own ending, without his having any more the religious faith of his upbringing, he still lived for the undying cause that would continue its future after him.

James had always known how it might end for the committed souls. Yet perhaps the end—in death, with only at best a partial fulfilment of a life's ideal—was not quite of that utterly final importance it seemed. To James, for all the vital importance of outcomes, it was also the bird on the wing that mattered, not the perch. 'I believe', he had said, in 'real possibilities, real indeterminations, real beginnings, real ends, real evil, real crises, catastrophes, and escapes, a real God, and a real moral life, just as commonsense conceives these things' (Preface to *The Will to Believe and Other Essays in Popular Philosophy*). As a consequence:

> I find myself willing to take the universe to be really dangerous and adventurous, without therefore backing out...I am willing that

there should be real losses and real losers, and no total preservation of all that is.   (*Pragmatism*, lecture 8 'Pragmatism and Religion')

Was Du Bois' commitment, was James' teaching, to be called a success, or a loss, or to have any name—and by what measure or time-scale? And it is not as though this questioning hadn't been occurring all the way along—the feeling of a life contracting with sorrow, expanding with joy, implicitly asking: is this working, has it worked, will it work in future? Emotions, the rise and fall of them in the course of life, won't stay away from these questions of going well, doing worse, getting somewhere or not. In a simple world of accountancy, James had said in lecture 8 of *The Varieties of Religious Experience*, the sum of a life's pluses and minuses, the separate happinesses and the discrete sorrows, yields its total worth. Yet even that still ends in death. There was another imaginable sense of life for James, with a different measure and from a higher dimension, in which the sums were not so simple, in which a number of negatives might still not tip the scale. In that, perhaps there could and should be no final settling of the accounts. And yet still there were real losses.

*

Apart from all that he thought and envisioned, Du Bois was only one individual, hazarding his spirit in the field of social action and reform. How William James would have hated those words 'apart' and 'only'. But it was in that field and in that fight that people had to make themselves even more narrowly liable to hurt and to failure.

James was a reformer in mental fight, and it was hard to know how much and in what ways this would be more or less effective; to what degree it was a professor's avoidance of the practical or a thinker's foundation for it. What we do know is that whatever the field of committed endeavour, there was inherently no escape from fundamental risk and partiality. And for James individuals existed, each in their own configuration, to make flesh all the possible versions and combinations along that spectrum, the whole human world uncertainly working between success and failure, in everything from politics to religion, from family to philosophy.

Here is a vision of that jeopardy, close to James's own. It comes from a reader of Thomas Hardy offering a sort of parable for the risk of belief, in a novel of his own. Again it arises out of education. In this story John Lindsay, head of a college of further education, takes a moment to tell his family about a recent conversation he has had with a member of his staff:

> 'A little while back I was talking to a parson on my staff. He teaches philosophy. Dry little chap. We were just walking along the corridor together; we'd exchanged a word or two, when he said, "One of my students asked me what I'd do if I became convinced that there was neither a God nor an after-life, what I'd think of the way I'd spent my span, in churches, in prayer, in alleged communion with a non-existent being. And I said, 'Young man, I would not regret one minute, because man must be serious and this is the way I was taught. It's as if I'd spent my life working on some branch of mathematical physics, and then found my theories superseded. I could not help feeling disappointed. I'm human. But I would not regret it, because I had done my serious best.'" And with that he turned off into a room.'

Lindsay pauses; his wife and daughter wait for the purpose behind this:

> 'For me,' John said, 'the belief would have been more important than my seriousness.'

Again a pause, and then further explication:

'If I'd practised something all my life, and found it wrong, I'd be shattered never mind how serious I'd been.'

This is from chapter 15 of a novel, *Still Waters* published in 1976 by a novelist I quoted in my previous chapter, Stanley Middleton, winner of the Booker Prize a couple of years earlier. He was also a Nottingham schoolmaster, my own teacher, from whose mix of teaching and writing I began to learn what literary thinking might be. In this little image from his work there are these two different voices or centres. One: 'I would not regret it, because I had done my serious best.' Two: 'If I'd practised something all my life and found it wrong, I'd be shattered.'

The first voice could be that of Du Bois, thrown out of America, still fighting the disillusionment and failure. Or what George Eliot might want to say on behalf of her own struggling people. But the second belongs with the sinking, shattering presence of the writer who represented what Middleton himself most feared to feel: Thomas Hardy. It was Middleton who first read to me Hardy's poem 'The Darkling Thrush', in the cold of the new year at the beginning of the twentieth century:

> At once a voice arose among
>   The bleak twigs overhead
> In a full-hearted evensong
>   Of joy illimited;
> An aged thrush, frail, gaunt, and small,
>   In blast-beruffled plume,
> Had chosen thus to fling his soul
>   Upon the growing gloom.
>
> So little cause for carolings
>   Of such ecstatic sound

> Was written on terrestrial things
> >   Afar or nigh around,
> That I could think there trembled through
> >   His happy good-night air
> Some blessed Hope, whereof he knew
> >   And I was unaware.

Those last two lines are the two voices again. But Hardy cannot turn that final line into the penultimate one, or make the penultimate the more affirmatory last word. Middleton himself was a hidden man, who in both his reading and his writing used literature reticently as a way of sending out messages he would not want to utter more directly. I now think he lived his life as if fought out between those two last lines. He said to me, when he first read me the poem, that in age Hardy had looked like that bird, 'frail, gaunt and small'; that the old man was moved by what the thrush could manage, in incongruous beauty, and he a human could not; and yet could not believe in a bird's apparent hope, even supposing a bird could sing from such a thing. 'So *little* cause…That I *could* think…there *trembled* through…Some blessed *Hope*' ('What a struggle,' muttered Middleton): '*he* knew | And *I* was unaware'. Hardy could not write the lines that the seventeenth-century poet George Herbert could, said Middleton, as he came out of the soul's dark night he had never expected to survive: 'And now in age I bud again, | After so many deaths I live and write; | I once more smell the dew and rain, | And relish versing' ('The Flower'). 'Who would have thought my shrivel'd heart | Could have recovered greenness?' wrote Herbert: not Hardy, for one. Middleton in his talk and in his writing would quote instead Hardy's 'I look into my glass': an old man looking in the mirror, wishing that, for peace's sake, his heart's still powerful feelings had grown as worn as the skin on his face: 'But Time, to make me grieve / Part steals, let part abide':

> And shakes this fragile frame at eve
> With throbbings of noon-tide.

It did not fit, the emotions had no place in such a body, in such a world. It was not as it was for Du Bois, that the darkling thrush could take human form in the music of the spirituals, the sorrow songs of lamenting belief that were like Psalms in their cries and prayers. But there were still, for Hardy, the poems he managed to get out. And yet towards the end of his life, Hardy wrote something that again Stanley Middleton read to me, thinking of himself too I believe: that though he, Thomas Hardy, had done all that he had meant to do, 'he did not know whether it had been worth doing' (*TH Life*, p. 478).

A story such as Du Bois' could only end for Hardy with the thought that, had it been he, he would have been shattered, never mind the seriousness of effort or its collateral benefits. No matter what an unknown future might or might not hold at some unspecifiable point, long after he'd have been there to see it. Hardy himself had imagined reform and the life of a social reformer without the formal dignity of that name. What his obscure reformer had set his life by was in retrospect an illusion, and always really had been, from the first. His young Jude, a poor boy, had seen Oxford on the horizon, and resolved to learn Latin and Greek, to try to get there. He had thought there would be one great rule, one rational law, by which to translate from one language to another. He finds there is instead only the long hard slog of learning word for word:

Somebody might have come along that way who would have asked him his trouble, and might have cheered him by saying that his notions were further advanced than those of his grammarian. But nobody did come because nobody does…

Jude the Obscure (1896), Part 1, chapter 4

Those absences and negatives in that final sentence, the continuous present tense at the last, the paradoxical grammar of non-happening—these are Hardy's black holes in the cosmos. In such a world his Jude was, in James's phrase, a real loser. He gets to Oxford but never to the university. His teacher exists only in his own head, in private reading. It is John Stuart Mill, encouraging individual experiments in life to create a more flourishing future for human beings. The same Mill whose utilitarianism was like an English step-father to James's pragmatism, since James dedicated *Pragmatism* itself to the memory of Mill, out of a shared belief in achieving happier human ends. And yet without clear guides or traditional principles, Jude's own experiments, especially within sexual relationship, ended as every reader of Hardy bitterly knows, only in renewed pain and defeat, and final oblivion. 'I am in a chaos of principles—groping in the dark—acting by instinct and not after example,' says Jude nearing the end, 'Eight or nine years ago when I came here first, I had a neat stock of fixed opinions, but they dropped away one by one; and the further I get the less sure I am' (Part 6, chapter 1) Again it didn't work. It's true that Hardy wasn't Jude; but with Jude's death Hardy himself never wrote another novel.

Hardy was James's contemporary: Hardy 1840–1928, James 1842–1910. To James, it always had to be a person, a complex living individual psychology, not an abstract philosophical concept, that most registers the recalcitrance of the world and in feeling it, best represents the fact of human resistance even through the involuntary personal pain. That is how James defined 'seriousness', 'the willingness to live with energy, though energy bring pain' ('The Sentiment of Rationality'). This chapter now fills out Hardy's brief note of dissent against James, and imagines that grim challenge from life as embodied reluctantly in Hardy, shattered by Truth that does not work. At the end of Henry James' 'The Beast in the Jungle', John Marcher stands at the tombstone of the woman whom he had never sufficiently loved, and looks across to see by a neighbouring grave a genuine mourner, one of the deeply stricken, with the deep ravages of suffering on his face. The mourner turns that face to Marcher, as if Marcher somehow profaned the air there, for not being the real thing. There are, the face says, 'real losses'. After *Jude*, Hardy found a way of continuing writing by turning increasingly to the crafting of small personal poems, the greatest of them those written in 1912–13 immediately after the death of his wife, Emma. But in that, Hardy was like a cross between Marcher and the mourner: he knew he had first loved Emma, but had also long since ceased to care, and now felt the two feelings together. There was no dignity, no abstract philosophy in it. 'In this real world of sweat and dirt, it seems to me that when a view of things is "noble", that ought to count as a presumption against its truth' (*Pragmatism*, lecture 2, 'What Pragmatism Means'). Hardy's challenge was not noble. But if Thomas Hardy turned his suffering face towards William James, how could Henry James's older brother meet the sort of pain that Hardy represented?

If the beauty of a straggling bird's song offered hope, something of that hope must also have come sub-consciously to Hardy from himself, from what in *The Mayor of Casterbridge* he called an 'outer chamber of the brain in which thoughts unowned, unsolicited...are sometimes allowed to wander for a moment prior to being sent off whence they came (chapter 42). But it is James the psychologist who says to Hardy what Hardy probably always knew but would never quite say: that his was *not* simply a psychological problem, a perverse twist or flaw, but really a religious problem:

> Pessimism is essentially a religious disease. In the form of it to which you are most liable, it consists in nothing but a religious demand to which there comes no normal religious reply.
>
> ('Is Life Worth Living?')

In his bereavement Hardy stood looking at a part of the garden when his wife worked at her planting, and almost believed she was still at his shoulder, throwing a shadow on the plot of ground in front of him. Stranded he cries, 'I am sure you are standing behind me' but 'There was no sound but the fall of a leaf / As a sad response' ('The Shadow on the Stone'). There comes no reply to the desperate faith.

William James had half-open secrets about the wager involved in trying to believe, which he made only as explicit as he had to.[14] I mean: the secret risk of believing that unhappiness might actually be useful and welcome, especially when it couldn't quite feel like that; or daring to think that unfairness, lack of moderation, even self-deception might be more useful for such as Luther than a saner norm; or how hope and desire might get from themselves the belief to be something of what they looked for.

Perhaps there is a God, but one who operates only through our own version of whatever god is. Or perhaps there is not, and we can only seek to represent in ourselves what we wanted Him to be to us, that otherwise was absent from the world. It could be either way, for William James.

This is how his thinking goes for me, in my translation. Suppose for me God is like '*this*' (whatever 'this' is in my case, say Merciful)—and suppose also that in the end He is not, or not existent at all—still, what I have done is bring 'this', the quality of mercy, into life as a by-product. A by-product which I probably could not have offered without the reassurance that it wasn't just me—though actually it may well have been. But it wasn't a 'me' I could otherwise have accessed or harnessed more directly; though I don't quite know why. That is to say, we think we need what we cannot wholly have: namely, external or higher validation for a true sense of meaning and vocation. But it may be we only need, or can only have, an *imagination* of such sanction, psychologically, to be able to create what we then depend upon.

If that is so, we can hardly at once exercise that imagination *and* be openly conscious that that *is* what we are doing, without returning ourselves to a sense of its being mere fiction or fantasy. But James thinks that we can be agnostic, just follow what may or may not be our imagination, in what seems to be getting us somewhere. And it may be it simply does not matter, when we cannot know for sure. What we can do for ourselves—even if we have call that God (or whatever), and even if it is God—we do in whatever ways we find we have to. And maybe that is how a strange withdrawn god wants it.

But—and this is perhaps the biggest point—these are thoughts that, in our limitation, we can't really think. Not in practice. That is why they have to be unspoken, or more or less in the background, so as not to be exposed to the air as hubris, silly and tortuous, tricksy and cheating. They are secrets that could cease to be so only if for once on some occasion they happened to become justified by event, the risk of delusion disappearing into the good fortune of their substantiation.

James had said no philosophy could ever be accepted that left human beings unable to feel or to act. Not pessimism if it 'essentially baffles and disappoints our dearest desires and most cherished powers'; not nihilism if it so contradicts 'our active propensities' as to give them 'no object whatever to press against'; not any philosophy that was 'so incommensurate with our most intimate powers as to deny them all relevancy' ('The Sentiment of Rationality'). And in a way Hardy agreed from the opposite side, like James in unhappy reverse: it *was* emotionally and almost biologically impossible for him to believe fully in the pessimism that should at least have saved him from continual disappointment. Some 'blessed hope' came in, even when he could not accept it. Hardy called pessimism 'the sure game' because it avoided the risk and vulnerability of hope (*TH Life*, p. 333). And yet whenever it mattered he could not play safe or feel sure. He could not accept even his own sense of meaninglessness. It wasn't just that his gloomily home-made philosophy did not work; his feelings themselves did not work in the world but kept on as if they might. So Hardy was like a pragmatist in giving room, however reluctantly, to emotions and needs that could not be denied. And yet they still did not go right, and, worse, they turned against the man who had them. So Hardy twists and turns in 'The Shadow on the Stone' to prevent it ending like 'The Darkling Thrush': 'I thought her behind my back' but 'I would not turn my head to discover / That there was nothing in my belief'—where 'would not' fights against 'noth-ing', in Hardy's double negatives:

> Nay, I'll not unvision
> A shape which, somehow, there may be.

Not only was Hardy, like a divided self, split in two in a way that James did everything to surmount; but the two opposites held him tensely together between them. He could neither believe in his feelings nor discard them. There *was* nothing in my belief: he could almost see it, see that nothing. Yet there was also that 'some-how may be'. He almost could hear it:

> Woman much missed, how you call to me, call to me,
> Saying that now you are not as you were
> When you had changed from the one who was all to me,
> But as at first, when our day was fair.   ('The Voice')

It would not be the same had he written, more safely, instead of 'you call', 'she seemed to call'. He felt he was haunted by her mem-ory not just inside but, almost madly, outside him What Hardy's rhymes hold and contain is what James describes as

> a zone of insecurity in human affairs in which all the dramatic interest lies: the rest belongs to the dead machinery of the stage. This is the formative zone… ('The Importance of Individuals')

In that zone, the poetic lines themselves mark the series of changes through a life—from the fair beginning to the mid-marriage alienation, and a final too-late repentance that almost brings the first times back—till Hardy then adds in a new stanza:

> Can it be you that I hear? Let me view you, then…

—in his self-division, the rationalist in him seeking some sensible proof. Those shifts, across lines and stanzas, as across times and feelings, are like the insecure movement of brain waves, of mental pathways within Hardy's verse. The hard-rhymed poems set up a force field in which each stanza marks the movement into a different sub-field—so to start a third stanza:

Or is it only the breeze, in its listlessness

'Or only': that is the sudden Hardyesque break of any faith in his own 'as if'. Poems like this, in ways that James would have understood with his feelings of 'if' and 'and' and 'but', hardly ever *name* the emotions as guilt or sorrow or love or regret but are the more intensely and inwardly emotional by means of the little words like 'or' and 'only'. They are even called now by linguisticians 'pragmatic markers', words that do not change the actual, basic propositions in a sentence but inserted within the grammar mark the personal, emotional difference even in passing. 'Or is it only the breeze?': the *breeze* not the *voice*, '*it*' not '*you*', the one he cannot yet bear to call 'she' or 'her', who was '*all*' to me, and now is '*only*' instead. These tiny words and their subtle inner relations are the minute molecular forces of pain working through the crannies of the verse, of which James wrote to Sarah Whitman, undermining hard positions and willed stances. 'Like pent-up water it will find a chink of possibility' (*TH Life*, p. 222).

Thomas Hardy's poetry has just these invisible molecular forces, in the undignified and ignoble world of commonplace sweat and dirt. His poems never had a great philosophy or esoteric myth to underpin or protect them, as did so much modernist poetry of the same era. They had to defend their everyday vulnerability through the power of strong language and strong rhyming structures holding onto what often seemed no more than non-events. Yet it was all that did not happen or did not work that nonetheless got under Hardy's skin. It is like the poem 'A Commonplace Day' when at the end of a day in which nothing bad happened, Hardy still finds himself inexplicably gloomy— as if something good that should have been, had somewhere

> missed its hope to be
> Embodied on the earth.

And there in that microscopic space between 'be' and 'Embodied' is the silent, invisible gap where life should have come. That is the zone of insecurity. There it shook Hardy that even in the mind of someone he cared about, he was no more than a thought, and a passing one: 'I am now but a thought of hers, / I enter her mind, and another thought succeeds me that she prefers' ('Wessex Heights'). And yet almost at the same time the thought of the woman possessed him like a separate presence, as if he was being driven out of his mind even by the thoughts of her within it.

The psychologist in James knew these shifts. He knew how suddenly, in the midst of connection, the barrier between my mind and yours feels again like 'the most absolute breach in nature' (PP 1, p. 226, chapter 9, 'The Stream of Thought'). Or how diminished I am, says James, when for example I feel shame, vulnerability or social discomfort. 'When I perceive my image in your mind to have changed for the worse', then I feel that 'something in me to which that image belongs' also changes. What 'a moment ago I felt inside of me, big and lusty' is 'now weak, contracted and collapsed' (PP 1 pp. 321–2, chapter 10, 'The Consciousness of Self'), and I am little and powerless again.

But Hardy himself wanted to be like a simple provincial countryman of common sense for whom things were either past or present, felt or unfelt, dead or alive, either here or there. Only, in his writing he hardly knew where he was. The boundaries of his reality kept moving and morphing. So, he looks at a chart of his genealogy in the desk in front of him and suddenly it turns into a map of his own brain, behind his eyes ('The Pedigree') His own words, like his own feelings and his own memories, turned back on him; the very sight of them hurt him, shaking this fragile frame. It was somewhat for him as it was for his self-repressed character Boldwood—to casual observers a model of stolid dependability, but inside perilously balanced between 'enormous antagonistic forces—positives and negatives in fine adjustment':

> His equilibrium disturbed, he was in extremity at once. If an emotion possessed him at all, it ruled him; a feeling not mastering him was entirely latent. Stagnant or rapid, it was never slow. He was always hit mortally, or he was missed.
>
> (*Far from the Madding Crowd*, chapter 18)

With Hardy the self had had to become so protective that the soul could hardly get out, except through temporary explosions of emotion and memory bursting through their rationalized containers, except as a sort of projected ghost he could hardly admit.

'We are all to some degree oppressed, unfree', wrote James in 'The Energies of Men', 'We don't come to our own. It is there but we don't get at it. The threshold must be made to shift.' Hardy's poems do show that threshold shifting, from the trigger of mundane events releasing his past losses and misses; they hold the resulting energies within them, as a field of vision and feeling. As Hardy put it in *The Return of the Native*, 'Persons with any weight of character carry, like planets, their atmospheres along with them in their orbits' (book 1 chapter 3). James himself could not have put it better. Hardy's poems are Hardy's little orbs and planets, his hurtling rockets or implosive time-bombs, carrying their own atmosphere or slipstream, their own memory, alive and resonant in the fringes of meaning. Hardy did not grow, he waited. He waited for whatever it was, however painful, that triggered his powers, beneath his default defences. But he could only do it from his past, not towards any future.

What most breaks open his defences is not so much an 'as if', as its past tense, 'what if'. In the poem 'Your Last Drive', what if his wife had known it was her last drive-out that day, a week before her death? What if he had accompanied her then, instead of his all too habitual refusal? What if she had been able to warn him how afterwards he might miss her, as he had not done for so long before? And even within this impossible imagination which tries to rescue the memory of what did *not* happen, she still returns the man to the realism of 'too late':

> 'You may miss me then. But I shall not know
> How many times you visit me there,
> Or what your thoughts are, or if you go
> There never at all. And I shall not care.'

It is an amazing series of mental flips and somersaults: to turn his thought of her into her thought of him; and then, even in that, the thought she has of the uselessness of his thinking of her. And to all this—which she *didn't* say, in relation to what she *wouldn't* know, and to what would be of *no use* anyway, three times over—he still replies, albeit to a ghost which is in truth 'only' projected from inside his own psyche. But psychology as explanation is for Hardy almost an admission of defeat—defeat of religion and of the psychic research into ghosts that William James would not give up on; defeat of meaning; defeat of the reality of her voice and of her very life. And still he cannot help speaking, steadily:

> True: never you'll know. And you will not mind.
> But shall I then slight you because of such?
> Dear ghost, in the past did you ever find
> The thought 'What profit', move me much?
>
> ('Your Last Drive')

It was that last line that told of how Hardy could not help defying its own denial. He has also written it as 'did you ever find / Me one whom consequence influenced much?' But 'move me much' is better: Hardy could not help being moved, was helplessly unmoved by arguments against useless emotions which nonetheless he kept on having. It is, I am saying, like James back-to-front, through the looking glass, from the negative or the other side.

Hardy is like a nightmare with almost everything coming out the wrong way round; even like the nightmare I had once about (of all things) Matthew Arnold's poem 'Empedocles on Etna' which I had taught many times. It was a poem Arnold never republished after its first appearance in 1852 because he felt it was too hopeless, all its action going into sad passivity. Phrases stuck in my head that night: 'Born into life! —'tis we / And not the world, are new', 'Limits we did not set / Condition all we do', 'To tunes we did not call our being must keep chime'. And in the nightmare, I just could not turn these words round; I could not make the sentences less passive or negative, less entrapping or more straightforward. 'To shift the structure of a sentence alters the meaning of that sentence, as definitely and inflexibly as the position of a camera alters the meaning of the object photographed. People know about camera angles now, but not so many know about sentences.'[15] I could not turn it around. And Hardy could only just about do so: 'I would not turn my head to discover / That there was nothing in my belief.'

In all this, there was something that James knew which Hardy himself had to acknowledge in his own way, in the thick of things: 'The only escape from faith is mental nullity' ('The Sentiment of Rationality'). Hardy could not escape to live in mental nullity or neutrality—'That there was nothing'—nor emotionally accept meaninglessness without feeling. But as with the self and soul, he could hardly live with the faith either, or even the hope of it. Nor could he accept what would have seemed to him any form of cheating, which he would have been all too tempted to adopt, if only he could have done so unconsciously.

*

The easiest but least interesting thing would be to say that in his cursory look Hardy mis-read William James. Repeatedly James went to considerable lengths to defend his shorthand proposition that 'truth is what works'. He said himself, 'How about the notorious fact that errors are so often satisfactory? And how about the equally notorious fact that certain true beliefs may cause the bitterest dissatisfaction?' (*The Meaning of Truth*, chapter 8 'The Pragmatist Account of Truth'). In answer to those objections, James included within the very criterion of 'what works' a double criteria: that a thought seeking to be true must have some agreement both with other internal thoughts and with external reality. 'There can be no truth if there is nothing to be true about'

('The Pragmatist Account of Truth'). The feeling of reality (called 'about') constrains what we can call true; it is not just left to human fantasy. We try out the descriptions most related to our need, in order to see how far, through trial and error in the midst of things, they can fit both us *and* the surrounding field. But Hardy found that he did not belong, his feelings did not fit. 'And nothing is much the matter; there are many smiles to a tear; / Then what is the matter is I, I say. Why should such a one be here?...' ('In Tenebris II').

It made Hardy treat James as if James was what he became in the hands of Wallace Stevens, the Harvard-educated poet of 'supreme fictions'. Hardy at some level hated the fictional, as a form of cheating. He came to poetry from his hard prose fiction, from fiction that had to destroy the fictive illusions within it: so it was with Tess, and Henchard and Jude. And his poetry had still to contain fact. 'True, never you'll know... Yet abides the fact, indeed, the same', 'Well, well, All's past amend / Unchangeable. It must go', 'Well, time cures hearts of tenderness, and now I can let her go'.[16] And still something inside Hardy that was emotionally counter-factual, could not be killed, kept coming back to life like memory itself. Like a walk and a climb with his young wife to be, decades ago: 'It filled but a minute. But was there ever / A time of such quality...?'. To one mind never:

> What we did as we climbed, and what we talked of
> Matters not much, nor to what it led, –
> Something that life will not be balked of...   ('At Castle Boterel')

'Nor to what it led' contains the future unhappiness of the marriage, but it is like 'Did you ever find / The thought "what profit?" move me much?', denying the cruder pragmatism of outcomes that Hardy thought was James's.

And though Hardy cries 'Yet — yet —' as at the end of a poem such as 'The Photograph', for James potential and possibility went further than a last-ditch hoping-against-hope. For James it was as though what was deeply felt as missing was pressing for its existence, and doing so with a power that even a profoundly felt disappointment like Hardy's did not fully allow:

> And if needs of ours outrun the visible universe, why *may* not that be a sign that an invisible universe is there?...God himself, in short, may draw vital strength and increase of very being from our fidelity.
> ('Is Life Worth Living?')

Hence James's interest in mysticism and psychical research, in the outside possibility of ghosts and the use of seances. Hence, even more, the extraordinary idea that H. G. Wells most relished in James, as his friend and master: that God or whatever we call some force for good in the universe, might be finite and need human help.

When Wells eventually writes of that idea in his prose tract, *God the Invisible King* (1917), it seems a too self-consciously quirky belief, and one he later repudiated. But when it first occurs in the novel *Mr Britling Sees It Through* (1916), it is different, coming like 'a thing as great as the first day of creation' to a man who has just lost his son in the madness of the First World War. And this man Britling, a writer who now sees how weak, silly, and rhetorically superficial all his previous writing has been, suddenly feels 'behind his eyes, and in his brain and hands' what had previous been only an idea. Namely: that the real god was closer to a Christ than to a God Almighty—was 'poor, mocked and wounded', and in need of our support as agents, even against our own sorrow, pain and evil (*Mr Britling Sees It Through*, book 3, chapters 1 and 2). That is why

Du Bois said, 'He was poor and we are poor; He was despised; He was persecuted and crucified, and we are mobbed and lynched.'[17] This is thought at its best only when *first* thought, or thought again as if for the first time, so as to be 'all that the thought thinks, exactly as the thought thinks it', uttered 'with every word fringed and the whole sentence bathed in that original halo of obscure relations' (*PP* 1, p. 276, chapter 9, 'The Stream of Thought'). It is that which matters in its origins—in the fringe, the obscure background—before it becomes established and repetitive, or too well knows its place. That doesn't mean that any passing fancy should be accepted, and nothing turns out to be nonsense, or that consolidation into an idea that can then be tested in the cold light of day is not an important part of an adult process of reasoning. It means only that something is likely *there* in an exciting original thought: there is as we say '*something in* it', an inkling which seeks the right place for itself, but may only take on a ludicrous appearance and lose its potential when spelt out wrongly. Then it is lost and denigrated for the while until its force is tried for again in a different time, context, or formulation. There was always in James the vital possibility of what he called 'wild facts', without stall or pigeon-hole, which in their flight 'threaten to break up the accepted system' ('What Psychical Research Has Accomplished'). Where Hardy can and will only write, 'A shape which, somehow, there may be', James says in words seeking to break into a parallel universe, 'Why *may* not that be...?'

Hardy would have his own answer to that. Possibilities, possibilities, endless possibilities: for him they hurt by what they enticed; they couldn't be forever sustained or always realized. There may be no clear boundaries in human existence, and yet there is still some point when people are forced back into their bodies and their circumstances; when the felt dualism of 'this' inside and 'that' outside returns, and there is real loneliness and loss and separation.

Once James overheard a seemingly chance remark by 'an unlearned carpenter of my acquaintance'. It was, as so often, just a single sentence:

> There is very little difference between one man and another; but what little there is, *is very important*.   ('The Importance of Individuals')

There is not much difference: 'we are not a bit elated', James goes on, 'that our friend should have two hands and the power of speech.' *That* a human being is able to speak at all leaves us cold, we take general capabilities for granted; it is *What* someone says, the small remark that a particular person makes out of that general capability which may be disproportionately electrifying. The large-scale biological human attributes remain only a steady base to work from; as fundamentals they themselves don't change. It is the smaller scale that matters more for us: it is those individual minute behavioural movements, including a mere word or two, that can activate and alter the general template and which count as life for us, according to our interests and emotions. Within this 'range of variation', the difference between Hardy and James, the movement from one to the other, is vital.

But this is of course also 'my William James' and 'my Thomas Hardy', most of all in the relation between them that forms itself in the mind. That means this: their existence as figures, as representative thoughts, as different centres of gravity, within the zone of insecurity of a reader who is somehow drawn to both, to their differing re-compositions of the same basic DNA that I have here tried to sketch. Between them they form a zone of experimental thinking where *in* both, and *between* each, there is a struggle to get the right things out of their wrong places, and into a better situation.

And yet for me, even in the conflict and tension, it is still not simply a case of either Hardy or James. It is true that as Emerson said of our moods, our authors often do not believe in each other. And it is possible to imagine those great splits where one of them must win and the other be exorcized, that subsequently a person might live on as more of a whole. D. H. Lawrence's 'Study of Thomas Hardy' is written in 1914, I think, to shed from Lawrence any retarding trace of what Hardy meant to him, to become his own Lawrence in the making. But I am saying that, instead of Hardy *versus* James as opposite centres of mental gravity, the one can turn swiftly into the other and back again in the struggles of a life. I think I have known when, in life and on page, my Middleton turned from Herbert into Hardy and could not get out again, or I here with my other two.

And this is again more as James himself described it: 'Philosophies are intimate parts of the universe, they express something of its own thought of itself' (A *Pluralistic Universe*, chapter 8, 'Conclusions'). Virtually, they are all there, the possible thoughts and the different systems, simultaneously. But within the world's range of the possible, each philosophy, and each unformalized embodiment of it in a person, becomes more or less emotionally relevant at different times and in different situations, in alternating seasons of purpose and of pain. 'Why, after all, may not the world be so complex as to consist of many interpenetrating spheres of reality, which we can thus approach in alternation...? (VRE, p. 100, lecture 4, 'The Religion of Healthy Mindedness').

'Interpenetrating' there is even more powerful than simply alternating. For in terms of the interpenetration of one thing within another, in terms of a shift in the field responsive to different thoughts and changed moments of emotional experience, it seems to me to go something like this: that the borders between Hardy and James, and what they stand for, are porous; that one can change into another, be lost or rescued in a moment, in the zone of insecurity. Just move the point, as John Jay Chapman urged, perhaps even by a fraction. It means that the Thomas Hardy in William James was *that it might not work*; but the William James in Thomas Hardy was *something that life will not be balked of*, too strong to be wholly denied.

'MENTAL DRAMA'

In 1896 William James spent a holiday at the Assembly Grounds, Chautauqua Lake, a resort made for ease and culture, for education, sport and the appreciation of natural beauty. It was a 'middle-class paradise', he said, 'without a sin, without a victim, without a blot, without a tear': 'a foretaste of what human society might be, were it all in the light, with no suffering and no dark corners' (*Talks to Students*, 'What Makes a Life Significant').

But when he left after a week and returned back home, what surprised him was a feeling of relief. On second thought, the order had been 'too tame', the culture too easy to be other than 'second-rate', the goodness 'too uninspiring'. He had re-crossed a mental border: it was no longer paradise but only 'Sabbatical city'. There was no battle for life there in Chautauqua, where victory was 'reduced to its bare chance'. This was the side of James that still wanted the 'lawless', 'precipitous', and 'intense'.

He told his young audience how, in re-action, he had found himself contrasting the retreat's comfort with the everyday world of common labour and the unrecognized efforts of working people. In the same way, his beloved Tolstoy had contrasted bourgeois intellectual artificiality with the more fundamental peasant realities recognized within the realism of the nineteenth-century novel: the importance of a slowly eaten piece of bread, the rhythmic work of the scythe in the fields, the quiet physical kindness offered at a sickbed.[1] 'Where now is *our* Tolstoi?' asked James.

But then James told the audience that he had found himself having to think again. As the second wave died down, he could see in it the privilege of nostalgic Romanticism. The appreciation of the unsung hero in the fields had in it too much sentimental over-correction—not in Tolstoy himself, but in Tolstoy at second hand. The dirt and sweat of toiling in the fields, he told the mainly well-to-do students in his audience, is not going to be for you a solution to what makes life significant, any more than joining the army. You will have to do your hard, brave work at a different level, and that begins with consciousness, with ideas and ideals.

But he added two further points. First, to have any genuine force, ideals could not be mechanically inherited or learnt by rote at camp or college. They had to feel alive and if not wholly original, at least feel vitally new, primary again, to take a hold of their thinker. And second, even then, that too was insufficient if those ideals were not channelled back into the world, to have a real effect out there. You are not here to become part of the PhD machine, he told his audience. Every time a sudden feeling evaporates without action or effect is a moment lost. The young need to know how soon, without taking those moments and turning them into a future and a character and a life, we become mere walking bundles of set habits, finished by the age of twenty-five.

I suggest that, once again, we now count the thoughts, and their phases, in this talk: (1) idyllic; (2) no, too tame; (3) better, rough labour; (4) *except* that could be too sentimental; (5) better, the forging of true not false ideals; *but* (6) they had to be thought anew; *and* (7) put into practice. Say, then, 7. But finally James admitted to his audience that for all its movements he found his own account here 'with all this beating and tacking on my part', too slow and laboured. It was suitable enough for an instructional lecture delivered to the young, a teaching story on the basis of past experience. But it was too steadily composed, delivered too much in retrospect and at second-hand, for a man who liked to think dramatically fast, without going through all the stages as though they were separate.

As I have tried to show throughout this book, they weren't simply as separate as they looked. In the reality of the temporal life into which we are thrown—

> No element *there* cuts itself from any other element, as concepts cut themselves from concepts. No part *there* is so small as not to be a place of conflux. No part there is literally *next* its neighbors; which means that there is literally nothing between; which means again that no part goes exactly so far and no farther; that no part absolutely excludes another, but that they compenetrate and are cohesive; that if you tear out one, its roots bring out more with them.
>
> (*A Pluralistic Universe*, lecture 6 'Bergson and
> his Critique of Intellectualism')

Yet still 'we name our thoughts simply, each after its thing, as if each knew its own thing and nothing else' (*PP* 1, p. 241, chapter 9, 'The Stream of Thought'). Hence, as we saw in Chapter 2, ordinary language cannot render the underlying, interpenetrating continuity of seemingly separate things, or the dynamic life that exists most of all in the flights and transitions that go on between more consolidated moments of thought. Even the word 'next' is a relative distortion when things flow into each other. 'Compenetrate' is the great word that James finds here.

This chapter makes one final move that takes 'my' William James into the literary genre that best shows his way of being, and best serves its transfer of understanding through readers into the world outside literature. One might have thought because of his interest in many-sidedness and the varieties of individual life that, as befitted the brother of Henry James, it would be the realist, psychological novel that best suited. The novelist Rebecca West wittily said that William James wrote philosophy as though it were a novel, while Henry James wrote fictions as if they were philosophy. And William James greatly admired the fusion of the two in the overflowing fullness of George Eliot's *Middlemarch*, in the simultaneity of the many interwoven lives there:

> The world is full of partial stories that run parallel to one another, beginning and ending at odd times. They mutually interlace and interfere at points, but we can not unify them completely in our minds. In following your life-history, I must temporarily turn my attention from my own. Even a biographer of twins would have to press them alternately upon his reader's attention.
>
> (Pragmatism, lecture 4, 'The One and The Many')

'But why always Dorothea?' writes George Eliot. 'Was her point of view the only possible one with regard to this marriage? (chapter 29). 'Mr. Casaubon, too, was the centre of his own world' (chapter 10). So the novel in its fullness makes its turns across different people, different dimensions, and different ways and forms of thinking to match them.

And yet, for all his admiration for the realist novel and its psychological width and depth, William James insisted that our best model for thinking about the world was not as 'readers only of the cosmic novel', but rather as actors:

> We are not the readers but the very personages of the world-drama. In your own eyes each of you here is its hero, and the villains are

your respective friends or enemies. The tale which the absolute reader finds so perfect, we spoil for one another through our several vital identifications with the destinies of the particular personages involved. (A *Pluralistic Universe*, lecture 2, 'Monistic Idealism')

We cannot long stand absolutely and impartially above and outside the imagined world, alongside a seemingly superhuman author such as George Eliot, giving tacit reassurance in the background. We are always getting involved inside the tissue of experience and there is no outside to it. 'Shall I commit this crime? choose that profession? accept that office, or marry this fortune?' The choice in the thick of things, says James, 'really lies between one of several equally possible future Characters'. It is not just what a person shall *do*. What a person 'shall *become*' is 'fixed by the conduct of this moment'. And even for seconds within such moments, 'the mind is at every stage a theatre of simultaneous possibilities' (*PP* 1 p. 288, chapter 9, 'The Stream of Thought').That is the drama of nascent and inchoate possibilities awaiting what form they may or may not take in whatever the specific context arising:

> There is thus a zone of insecurity in human affairs in which all the dramatic interest lies; the rest belongs to the dead machinery of the stage....
>
> The zone of the individual differences, and of the social twists which they initiate, is the zone of formative processes, the dynamic belt of quivering uncertainty, the line where past and future meet. It is the theatre of all we do not take for granted, the stage of the living drama of life. ('The Importance of Individuals')

This is what James wanted: dramatic lines of life-in-the-making, that instead of being separate, flowed into each other, moving backwards as well as forwards; lines that morphed and contorted and resolved themselves within the field they formed. In Shakespeare you could actually see these lines of life, in the script and the text, like a template underlying the activation of life on stage, such that character like thought and feeling came like an eruption.

Even at the closing down of Othello, when Othello no longer seems to have anywhere to go, no future, and no one to be but what he has now become, James sees a last desperate twist of life:

> What better way to rescue him at last from this debasement than to make him for an instant identify himself in memory with the old Othello of better days, and then execute justice on his present disowned body, as he used then to smite all enemies of the State?
>
> (PP 2, pp. 362–3, chapter 22, 'Reasoning')

Shakespeare did not slowly spell it out; in drama he did not have to know how or why he did it, but only do it and make it happen: 'That speech about the turbaned Turk suddenly simply flashed across him as the right end of all that went before' (p. 362). Othello cries out: 'in Aleppo once / When a malignant and a turbaned Turk / Beat a Venetian and traduced the state, / I took by th' throat the circumcised dog / And smote him thus' (Othello 5.2 348–52). 'And thus', in this blended past–present, stabs *himself* as though he were for a single instant both the righteous killer and the deservedly punished, in one. The last act in the theatre of *simultaneous* possibilities, it is what minutes later might be described for ever after as 'suicide'—as in the dead machinery of the stage; but in the moment of dramatic happening the killing of oneself is paradoxical. And significantly it is a *half* line, unfinished, that Othello ends on:

> I took by th' throat the circumcised dog
> And smote him thus.

—like a cue, a momentary space left to be filled by the cross-over into action. James honoured that interstitial space, 'the theatre of all we do not take for granted, the stage of the living drama of life' ('The Importance of Individuals').

Drama, and above all, I am arguing, the language of Shakespearean drama, offers a working model for James's sense of things, otherwise barely capturable, by embodying examples in spontaneous practice.[2] Raw, primordial, and originating energy, as of sub-atomic forces seeking embodiment, is of the essence here—for James, Shakespeare reiterates the original acts of creation: situations, worlds and times, words, thoughts, people suddenly coming into being. So it feels overwhelmingly to James in an unfiltered entry that he makes in his diary, on watching a performance of *Hamlet* at the very time of his own depressive sense of redundancy:

> April 13 [1868]. Good God! I never felt the might of it so before. The endless fullness of it— How it bursts + cracks at every slam....Is the mode of looking in life of wh. Hamlet is the expression a final one or only a mid stage on the way to a new + fuller classical one....The fullness of emotion becomes so superior to any possible words, that the *attempt* to express it adequately is abandoned, and its vastness is indicated by the slipping aside into some fancy, or counter-sense— so does action of any sort seem to Hamlet inadequate and irrelevant to his feeling.[3]

Hamlet is here like Shakespeare's proto-drama, the zone he creates in which to ponder what of surplus potential and excess can go into and what come out of its holding ground; what amidst the almost infinite possibilities can find finite words, action, character, and not be melancholically blocked and frustrated. Struggling for the right place for itself, the play seems to James not to know whether it is a dead end or an experimental middle. And there the mind of protagonist is, in James' phrase, the psychologist within and upon itself. In his own later work James remembers the crucial lines that express this feeling of uncertain predicament:

> And thus the native hue of resolution
> Is sicklied o'er with the pale cast of thought.   (*Hamlet* 3.1 83–4)

In *The Varieties of Religious Experience*, they mark the Hamlet-like moment when the fighting spirit of the moralist is exhausted, the athletic attitude to life breaks down, and, the world of effort insufficient, when 'morbid fears invade the mind': then 'to suggest personal will and effort to one all sicklied o'er with the sense of irremediable impotence is to suggest the most impossible of things'. For what the sick soul really craves is religious: 'to be consoled in his very powerlessness, to feel that the spirit of the universe recognizes and secures him, all decaying and failing as he is' (VRE, pp. 43–4, lecture 2 'Circumscription of the Topic'). In *The Principles of Psychology*, the Hamlet lines are again a trace-memory for the loss of motor-energy, the explosive impulsiveness that drove on 'the most successful military and revolutionary characters in history', the better for their 'hair-trigger organization, and for not being "sicklied o'er with the pale cast of thought"' (PP 2, p. 538, chapter 26, 'The Will'). That is how the play ponders the advantage and disadvantage of secondary inhibition, of consciousness itself in mental department 2, in comparison with the simpler primary drama of warrior fathers and military contemporaries. It struggles with the loss of firstness, in the death of the old heroic father:

'A was a man, take him for all in all.
I shall not look upon his like again.   (1.2 186–7)

and increasingly becomes a play dominated by a sort of Jamesian half-possible, half-baulked 'feeling of would', a conditional turning across the lines of still unsettled alternatives, or slipping into some counter-action: 'For who would bear the whips and scorns of time /...When he himself might his quietus make / With a bare bodkin? Who would fardels bear /...But that the dread of something after life /...puzzles the will' (3.1 69–77). And thus resolution is lost: Who would...*when* might; who would...*but that*: it is Shakespeare who most reveals the underlying in-betweens of thought that are part of the Jamesian grammar I discussed in Chapter 2.

The experimental psychologist in James loved the idea of being able to look into Shakespeare's 'nervous system'—which itself might be another name for the plays—to see how and why

> at a certain period of his life his hand came to trace on certain sheets of paper those crabbed little black marks which we for short-ness' sake call the manuscript of Hamlet.
> (*PP* 1, p. 132, chapter 5, 'Automaton Theory')

Those lines, those black marks. This would be something like what we now have in the neuro-science of brain-imaging, which James here calls 'body-history'. But running parallel to it is 'mind-history' or 'spiritual history', in which three pounds of brain take the form of a living, breathing, feeling creature full of meanings, requiring 'an account in which every gleam of thought and emotion should find its place' (p. 133). And for James, crucially, those two levels, micro and macro, not only are parallel but mutually affect one another, as though electrically conversing together through loops and feedbacks, translations, interventions and re-entries.

In Shakespeare, by reading you can see the diagram in the lines, before the code is activated from page to stage. That is how Shakespeare's language is like a template for new creation, the actors standing to their script as mind stands to brain, trying humanly to embody codes, messages, and needs. Shakespeare scanned and wired his lines so that if actors would map themselves onto what was there, it would be a dynamic template for life. As a psychologist, with a lab of his own, William James would have loved the way we can now try using brain-imaging on suddenly surprising verbal shifts to detect subliminal, interstitial, and microscopic effects within the very physiology of mind.[4]

A dramatic line is as near as we can get to capturing what James calls the snowflake crystal of thought amidst the heat of events. A line holds a transient thought, marking it permanently in the script, before serving also to release it forward into completed human sense: 'to die, to sleep— / No more—'

— to **die**: to **sleep** —

To **sleep**, *perchance* to **dream** — aye, there's the rub,

For in *that* **sleep** *of* **death** *what* **dreams** *may* come

When we have **shuffled** off this mortal coil

Must give us pause   (3.1 59–67)

In what is almost too much (as my added direction-lines, **bold** nouns and verbs, and connective *italics* indicate), the line is itself the major form of punctuation, whatever later editors put in by way of over-explicit commas and dashes to civilize the wild Shakespearean movements in code. Because really Shakespeare is bare, with no signals in the speed of writing and transition to show in advance quite where you are going. 'Erase the name of the speakers', said John Jay Chapman, 'and the text itself keeps them in place. Destroy stage directions, remove the stage, pull down the theatre, and yet the play goes forward: everything is expressed in the lines themselves.'[5] That is the dynamic and dramatic insecurity, *before* selves are known, or directions clear. The text has to be ridden, such that it is through its 'pauses' that thought happens, making a death into but a sleep, and yet a sleep into a dream, and then a dream back into a nightmarish-thought of death; turning a 'that' into a 'what', and even a 'may' into a 'must'. James would love the Shakespearian conjunctions, feeling their way: '*But that* the dread of something after death / . . .puzzles the will'

> And makes us *rather* bear those ills we have (*one line, one thought*)
> *Than* fly to others that we know not of (*next line, another thought*)
> (3.1. 80–1)

The lines are like cues, stage-directions saying to the actors as the people enacting them: Hold on by the lines as though they were your brain waves; turn mentally this way, now the other way, ride the shifts and pressures in the nervous system.

And as Chapman suggests, it is good when something of that improvised instability is retained unsmoothed in the theatre, with the actor still in the zone of insecurity. Originally, to save time and money, the actors were not given the whole text, just their own 'parts' and the rough cue of the last few words from the other actor to prompt them. In terms of what James calls partaking, or part-taking, the actors had to respond in the midst of experimental surprise, with decisions in the making and the moment. As characters both receive and provide a cue in the dramatic midst of time present, their mind *in situ* has to think: Where am I?—what is this outside thing that I have to take in?—what is to be done with it, inside?—how is it then to be given back in return?[6] It is like Hermione in *The Winter's Tale* when she says, in shock: as for my husband's love—

> I do give lost, for I do feel it gone
> But know not how it went.   (*The Winter's Tale*, 3.2 92–4)

In shifts like this across the lines, 'the abrupt transitions in Shakespeare's thought astonish the reader by their unexpectedness,' says James (*PP* 2, p. 362, chapter 22, 'Reasoning'). No sooner is something momentarily taken out of the stream, to give it thought, than it has to go back in again without time for its thinker to know quite how, why, or where 'it went'. It wouldn't work so powerfully, if the text were more straightforwardly linear and chronological: 'I know not how it went / But I do feel it gone'. In the Shakespearian movements lies James's own sense of pure existence: 'No element *there* cuts itself from any other element, as concepts cut themselves from concepts. No part *there* is so small as not to be a place of conflux.... They compenetrate and are cohesive.' The need to try to stop, to extrapolate and conceptualize, makes the stream seem to go even faster; discontinuity swallowed up within the speed and force of the on-going continuousness of time. The worth and interest of the world, says James, consists not in its separate elements but 'in the dramatic outcome of the whole process and in the meaning of the succession stages which the elements work out' (*A Pluralistic Universe*, appendix B, 'The Experience of Activity'). In that rushing process the play 'bursts + cracks at every slam', such that what James says of Shakespeare is what he most often says of the mind when most powerfully individual, most full, and most spontaneously dramatic, in life itself:

> Instead of thoughts of concrete things patiently following one another in a beaten track of habitual suggestion...we seem suddenly introduced into a seething cauldron of ideas, where everything is fizzing and bobbling about in a state of bewildering activity, where partnerships can be joined or loosened in an instant, treadmill routine is unknown, and the unexpected seems the only law.
>
> ('Great Men and Their Environment')

A wild cauldron of energies, creative and destructive, not a treadmill. 'Blow winds and crack your cheeks', shouts Lear, calling upon the bolts of lightning, 'You sulphurous and thought-executing fires / Singe my white head'; in himself invoking the all-shaking thunder to 'Strike flat the thick rotundity of the world' (*King Lear* 3.2 1–7). In that cauldron, words have to move at molten heat and adapt suddenly—from noun to verb, from adjective to noun, from present tense to conditional mood—in the light of something forcing its way through into the world, using whatever it can in order to come into being. James made those shifts himself when he wrote of '*a* more', or 'the eaches', or the 'ever not quite', or 'the doing of the fact', to create new ideas in new energies untamed by conventional grammar. In that storm of thought, James said, it is not first of all silence, and *then* the thunder, and *then* the lightning, but 'into the awareness of the thunder itself the awareness of the previous silence creeps and continues; for what we hear when the thunder crashes is not thunder *pure*, but thunder-breaking-upon-silence-and-contrasting-with-it' (*PP* 1, p. 240, chapter 9, 'The Stream of Thought'). Is this a dagger I see before me, asks

Macbeth, or a dagger of the mind? Is this storm inside my white head as well as outside it? Shakespeare will not let words and thoughts get subordinated to a taming grammar: the dramatic vocabulary will cross normal boundaries, the words will stay alive and be powers in their own right. The language is not 'about' the process, but with rough-handed speed it goes on *within* it, and it erupts out of it, to give sudden voice. It is what Robert Frost calls the 'kingly' departure from the norm in the 'Freedom to flash off into wild connections, / Once to have known it, nothing else will do'.[7]

Human nature is itself of that dramatic nature. In the lower creatures it is more automatic: 'Nature has left matters in this rough way, and made them act *always* in the manner which would be *oftenest* right'; but in the higher species, 'Nature implants contrary impulses to act on many classes of things, and leaves it to slight alterations in the conditions of the individual case to decide which impulse shall carry the day. Thus, greediness and suspicion, curiosity and timidity, coyness and desire, bashfulness and vanity, sociability and pugnacity, seem to shoot over into each other' (*PP* 2, p. 392, chapter 24, 'Instinct'). Out of that conflict of contradictory instincts and in that struggle for equilibrium, comes what is the drama of consciousness, not because the evolved human creature no longer has instincts but because it has so many. 'The whole drama is a mental drama' (*PP* 2, p. 564, chapter 26, 'The Will').

*

For a pragmatist the only thing that matters in choosing one word, one thing, one idea over another, is whether it makes any actual difference. What difference does this idea and sense of a dramatic life make to ordinary life? If it is essential to the vitality of life, can it be sustained or borne there, or must it be tamed and normalized? Any reader might think: my life is much more routine than James allows or would like, it isn't a medium for drama; most days, it does not have any forward movement or the privilege of a sense of new opportunity.

Hardy has a little poem called 'The Reminder'. It is a good title for a man frightened by casually looking over old letters and photographs, the time-bombs that could go off at any moment. This time he is sitting by a warm Christmas fire, feeling better than usual, when he happens to look out of the window and see in the harsh frost outside a thrush driven, in sharp distress, to trying to eat a rotten berry. Then comes another of his minor poetic heart attacks, as if in punishment for relaxing and lowering his guard:

> Why, O starving bird, when I
> One day's joy would justify,
> And put misery out of view,
> Do you make me notice you!

Just when he was happy, the unhappy part of him expelled…! This is about two movements of field-change. First, what we saw in the last chapter and again in this: that bounds are not as physical and separate as they appear but are porous. That means Hardy inside cannot seal off his feelings from the invasive plight of the bird outside, and there's a near-primitive feeling in the poetry belonging to an earlier emotional world, prior to the safe establishment of a separate ego. The bird is in him. That is the drama.

But secondly when Hardy at the end writes wryly to the bird, 'Why do you *make* me notice you!', it is the explanation mark that gives it away. Hardy does not really believe, does not rationally think that a weak starving bird could have 'made' him have these distressed feelings—though it emphatically felt that way. It is like when he thinks he hears his dead wife's voice, he still *has* to ask, 'Or is it only the breeze?' ('The Voice'). Isn't it 'only' a psychological projection, existent inside but non-existent without; projected onto the outside world, because the inside is of itself insufficient to be real? *Only* leaves you bereft, it is just you and your needy psychological illusions. And you may then have defensively to re-organize inside, so as to lessen the feel of loss. That is Hardy's characteristic second-thought movement into a second world that brings back the boundary again between within and without. It is impressive that Hardy can bear it and can at least make something, a poem, out of it. Otherwise, it might have driven Hardy beyond sanity. But it is still a loss of firstness, a sort of continuously renewed death into a separate self.

For Hardy, there is always some lost first world, some memory of an Eden, that haunts all our subsequent fallen emotions of broken hope, of disappointment and regret, even if that idyllic Eden never existed, and is only a back-formation of our pain crying that it should never have got like this. 'In the ill-judged execution of the well-judged plan', Hardy writes in *Tess of the d'Urbervilles*, 'Nature does not often reply '"Here" to a body's cry "Where?"'' (chapter 5). The original design for a good world, if ever there was one, is long since in broken ruins.

This is what Robert Frost is thinking about in his essay, 'The Figure a Poem Makes' where he says that every poem is an exemplar of how far a person can carry forward a first intent into a second phase of implementation. 'Be it in art, politics, school, church, business, love, or marriage', the terrible challenge is whether the 'original intention it had has been strongly spent or weakly lost'. Often the first life of the thing is lost or damaged rather than fulfilled through its test and trials: sometimes because it was ill-conceived and in genuine need of revision; sometimes because it was ill-timed and could not grow straight within an unpropitious context; but worst of all, when its energy is suppressed or dissipated even to the point of betraying and abandoning its original spirit. For James the meaning of morality lies in how far a good course is fought for and held onto by will, 'affirming and adopting a thought which, if left to itself, would slip away (*PP* 2, p. 565, chapter 26, 'Will'). The secondary travesty of this is if 'morality becomes a question of nicely educated people making choices between different courses of action and being able to account for them': then the tame and normal world becomes somewhat awful.[8] It's what was at stake when James' colleague in pragmatism, C. S. Peirce spoke of firstness and secondness in a paper 'On a New List of Categories', delivered to the American Academy of Arts and Sciences in 1867. Firstness is the original conception, free but fragile, vague but powerfully fresh. Secondness is its embodiment in existence, potential and possibility turned into actuality, the movement from the amorphousness of 'something' into the definiteness of *this*. For James, it was crucial that the second move carried forward the nimbus or resonance of the first inchoate intent, and did not settle down into a third state of inertia. In biography and history, he said, designs do have to be modified, pragmatically, 'to suit events which interfere with the original plan': 'lines of fulfilment' are always 'mixed with collaterals' and no plan was ever fully carried out 'by a single act of thought' or 'foretold in all its details' (MEN, p. 5). For Frost, writing was like striking 'a line of purpose' into a poem as into a landscape: the line cannot be 'mechanically straight', the path has always to be adapting to the ground; but instinctively we can sense how far we have stayed on course. Or to put it another way, there was a part of Frost that was always saying as if also to Thomas Hardy: 'Before I built a wall I'd ask to know / What I was walling in or walling out' ('Mending Wall').

*

A first world, a primarily dramatic world without walls, is what John Jay Chapman suggested that you get with Shakespeare: the raw first feel bursting out. Take away the names of the characters, the stage directions, the punctuation, the summary conceptions of character, the polished performance. These aids and labels are just like our normal protective selves, perched on the branch between flights.

Drama is, rather, what happens whenever—for example— instead of *two* separate people, a third thing is created in the space between them, like a grammatical conjunction, active but anonymous and invisible.

On one side, then, is Caesar Octavius, on the other Mark Antony, but Octavia, Octavius' sister made wife to Antony, exists precisely in the force-field between them, and for once visibly embodying that space, is torn within it. Or later, Octavius himself encounters Antony in battle, but now with Antony's own men, deserters who despaired of Antony's slavery to Cleopatra, on his side. It is not just about swelling the sheer numbers: rather, Octavius knows that for Antony it will feel as if those who have left him embody what he has lost of his very self, and weaken him further from within. 'That Antony may seem to spend his fury / Upon himself' (*Antony and Cleopatra*, 4.6 10–11). Antony had already felt this: 'Let that be left / Which leaves itself' (3.11 19–20). These quiet line-endings know that there is no space in reality too small for strange shifts in the field of being.

By the end, even his entrusted deputy, Enobarbus leaves Antony to join Octavius. Yet despite himself, Antony sends Enobarbus the treasure he has had to leave behind, with overplus, knowing the desertion was not simply external, separate, and undeserved: 'O, my fortunes / Have corrupted honest men' (4.5 16–17). Yet simultaneously across the stage, Enobarbus is left both feeling for Antony, as though Antony's ruin were part of himself, *and* separately blaming himself for adding to it. Both connected and cut off, Enobarbus cries out, though quite alone: 'O Antony, / Nobler than my revolt is infamous' (4.9 18–19). Through such complex inter-relations across boundaries, one whole thing is dramatically working itself out here, in every part of itself.

Or again, drama is what gets generated whenever with *one* person on stage, a second presence—the presence of that which is spoken *of*—is as existent in its verbal resonance as the person speaking it. There are invisible forces on stage here, coming and going. In *Macbeth*, medicine, cure and physic, sleep and peace and wholeness—all as though with capital letters—won't come in any more. 'Pity' and 'Remorse' will never quite leave the nightmare, no more than will 'Blood', despite the calls for 'Darkness' and 'Night'. 'Stop up th' access and passage', cries Lady Macbeth unavailingly, 'to remorse' (*Macbeth*, 1.5 42). 'But wherefore could I not pronounce "Amen"? / I had most need of blessing and "Amen" / Stuck in my throat' (2.2 34–6) says Macbeth, almost to himself. Thoughts and Qualities and Emotions and Dispositions are not abstractions here but feel like things in themselves, as real as the physical substances they mentally penetrate. 'The psychological agents in the drama', says James, are 'the ideas themselves': 'the ideas are themselves the actors, the stage, the theatre, the spectators, and the play' (*Talks to Teachers*, chapter 15, 'The Will'). The rule in Shakespeare is that to name a thing is momentarily to have to be it. These 'things' are as real in the play as the 'people' are: they are part of the people, the people are part of them. Energy in Shakespeare's cosmos takes whatever form it can have, human or non-human, dependent on opportunity and context. There is no time for a second world in which to rationalize and explain this, or translate it into what seems more normal.

But in ordinary life, or life made ordinary as James warned his students, human beings harden and slow and settle. Explanation seems to tame reality, and slow thinking is given high status, for seeming more considered and deliberate, and therefore more rational. But slow thinking for James all too often leads to the creation of false entities and abstract existences, destructive of the life of energy. Ponderous interpretation would say that James's pragmatism means he deliberately chose and set up ideas that then best enabled him to be happier or more active, and to justify doing what he wanted. That interpretation is slow thinking where 'slow' means a falsified world-view based on prior control and self-calculation, on nouns put into place like ducks in a row, rather than the Jamesian grammar of verbs coming into being. With James, thought creates and recreates its own thinker. The thinkers find themselves through their thoughts, their thoughts developing into persons. Where thinking is so tight-packed and so fast, the most important element is suddenly 'the mere feeling of a right or wrong direction in the thought' (*PP*, 1. p. 261). In the words of *Macbeth*, such intuition feels 'the future in the instant' (1.5. 56). This dramatic thought, by release of its compression into time, creates its thinker's unfolding movement into a future. It is like thinking for the first time, hitting upon an experientially forged thought that seems unexpectedly somehow to feel right, to clear and release the previously blocked way, and already be a part of an action.

I say 'already' because this is part of what James calls 'the whole drama of the voluntary' (*PP* 1, p. 453, chapter 11, 'Attention'): that there are not separate faculties but rather, changing phases of the same effort to become more alive in the world. 'Thinking' and 'striving' were only two different versions of it, in its struggle to be. Something felt, that was yet unclear but was looking for existence in the world, lived and expressed itself in the various interdependent modes of conception, attention, will, and act—each one of them a different re-presentation of the other at a particular moment in a particular place. 'Conception' became 'attention' as soon as it was held onto for more than a moment. And that attention both strengthened the conception and helped create forward from its use 'the will'. And the will turned intent itself into 'action', by a kind of transformative movement working throughout the continuously coursing current. The whole drama of the voluntary included the involuntary and the pre-voluntary in suddenly coming into release, the fringes reforming into a fresh nucleus. That emergent thought had not planned a way forward, in advance; rather the consciousness it urgently triggered felt more like a burst of dramatic revelation. That is what James meant by saying truth *happens* in the 'quest', a search not in the first place for some appropriate action but 'for the right conception' that opens up the possibility of action otherwise not yet known or existent (*PP* 2, p. 531, chapter 26, 'Will'). Then mental inhibitions, resistances, tangles and difficulties give way to something like 'the relief of a musician in resolving as confused mass of sound into melodic or harmonic order' ('The Sentiment of Rationality'). It is the agnostic or aesthetic moment when (we hardly know how) the actor or musician gets it right in performance, or the psychoanalyst offers a moment of cathartic release in treatment, or you manage a right word or action in an important conversation: something comes to life and falls into place that transforms the explicit score, the technical rule and theoretic concept, into a type of artistic practice and temporal accomplishment. And it is quick.

These potentialities for getting it right 'all lay embedded in the primordial chaos of sensations which gave the mere matter to the thought of all of us indifferently', ready for the next experimenter in life to create something out of it (*PP* 1, pp. 288–9, chapter 9, 'The Stream of Thought). This bubbling mass of matter is as it were waiting to be shaped, again and again, in what is a revolutionary reappraisal of what is truly 'higher' knowledge. It is not what has been classically thought for centuries, that the highest thinking is the most general, the most permanent, the most like fixed laws:

> Why, from Plato to Aristotle downwards, philosophers should have vied with each other in scorn of the knowledge of the particular, and in adoration of that of the general, is hard to understand, seeing that the more adorable knowledge ought to be that of the more adorable things, and that the things of worth are all concretes and singulars. The only value of universal characters is that they help us, by reasoning, to know new truths about individual things. The restriction of one's meaning, moreover, to an individual thing, probably requires even more complicated brain-processes than its extension to all the instances of a kind...
>
> (*PP* 1 pp. 479–80, chapter 11, 'Attention')

Out of all those manifold potentialities, and amidst other failures, it is the fusing together, the chemical combination of *this* moment, *this* individual, *this* act, *this* thought, out of the whole human background, that the emotionally unembarrassed James calls 'adorable'. This is the drama James loves, something creatively working itself out through the diverse potential characters of life, across the whole wide human stage, resulting this time, each time, in just one individual culmination. I have never felt the individual thing so uniquely valued.

I can't forget that dramatic spirit, that life, even when, frustrated or disappointed or bored, I cannot fully deploy it in the scope and terms of my own existence. And though I have tried to describe it here in order to call it back to mind, always, finally, there returns the question to be put to our own experience and to the world-memory of human experience that is held in literature: What does this dramatic view really feel like in life's more common and ordinary contexts? Can it still survive there? How can it, possibly? What in our mundane world, in the world of apparent second-ness, can it actually effect or become for us?

And this is where the realist novel may become useful again, serving as a halfway house in which to recommence that translation between the dramatic and the ordinary. The dramatic need might look something like this in a realist setting—where in the zone of insecurity, an orphan boy is only just recovering from a critical illness in the home of benevolent strangers:

> The old lady very gently placed Oliver's head upon the pillow; and smoothing back his hair from his forehead, looked so kindly and loving in his face…'What would his mother feel if she had sat by him as I have, and could see him now!'
>
> 'Perhaps she does see me,' whispered Oliver, folding his hands together; 'perhaps she has sat by me. I almost feel as if she had.'
>
> 'That was the fever, my dear,' said the old lady mildly.
>
> 'I suppose it was,' replied Oliver, 'because heaven is a long way off; and they are too happy there, to come down to the bedside of a poor boy. But if she knew I was ill, she must have pitied me, even

there; for she was very ill herself before she died. She can't know anything about me though,' added Oliver after a moment's silence. 'If she had seen me hurt, it would have made her sorrowful; and her face has always looked sweet and happy, when I have dreamed of her.'

The old lady made no reply to this

Charles Dickens, *Oliver Twist* (1837–8), chapter 11

Here it is, projection again, but not so much attempted expulsion of the feared or unwanted or miserable from within, as creation of the much wanted and much missed inside, made manifest out-side. But even here the *maybes*—of 'What would...if she could', 'Perhaps she does', 'I almost feel as if'—are met and dragged back behind the border by the *onlys*: 'That was the fever', 'I suppose so', and 'no reply to this'. Even in those reservations the old lady tacitly understands that the feverish boy has been seeing her as if she were his own mother, and she doesn't want wholly to disabuse him of that.

It is Oliver's mistake, Oliver's projection. It's the child's need for meaning and love, as if the two were the same. And even as it exposes our own psychological origins, the ordinary, secondary adult world must rationalize it away, as something in Dickens that is childishly over-dramatic and sentimental.

But I don't care what exactly the child thinks or just how accur-ately he copes with reality, only that he does so without losing heart, and does it inventively. I mean, Oliver thinks first of all that his dead mother may have been looking over him, even from heaven above. But then, he thinks, she would have had to feel, even in the happiness of heaven, the pain of helplessly pitying her child, knowing all she did about such illness from her own final experience of it. And yet, thinks Oliver through yet another turn: she can't know anything about me—and Dickens pauses here, as if at the absolute sadness of a disillusioning truth; but then going on to say something different—*not* that such claims are nonsense, but she can't know because when I thought she came to me in my dreams, she did not look sorrowful as she would have been to see me so poorly, but as sweet and happy as ever. What matters is not so much the so-called truth of any particular part of that content, but the creative mobility of mental life between each and any of them, which comes from the intelligence of his love and his need of being loved, and the preservation in some form of both, across the bounds and pressures of time and place and person. James himself hardly believed in projection as such, and certainly not as some separate attempt from within, cunningly to manipulate reality. He wrote: 'Subjective consciousness, aware of itself as subjective, does not at first exist. Even an act of pain is surely felt at first objectively, as something in space which prompts to motor reaction': Subjectivity and interiority, he added, come second, not first, and 'are the notions *latest* acquired by the human mind' (*PP* 2, pp. 32, 43, chapter 17, 'Sensation'). So-called projection was really what we almost always have to do, instinctively, in the world: react, try this out, make this incursion, get that response and feedback, re-set and attempt another overture. And it is not just expulsion or splitting or fantasy: it is trial and error, like bats registering the echoes from their own cries to create a sonic map. 'My action is the complement which, by proving congruous or not, reveals the latent nature of the mass to which it is applied' ('The Sentiment of Rationality'). It is a form of exploratory communication.

Losing a mother or needing love is there as a fact in the world. The real question is what has to be done with it, how it has to appear and adapt within many different modes and forms. *It*, as James might say, is the actor, looking for some way or someone to help play its part. Of children evacuated in war-time in 1940, Anna Freud, daughter of the great psychoanalyst, said that they

> experienced not their own, very real separation, but the imagined distress, loneliness and longing of the mother whom they had left behind. 'I have to telephone my Mummy, she will feel so lonely' was a frequent wish, especially in the evening.[9]

Again I don't care so much in the first place which way round it has to come out as: that's the drama and the insecurity, and the tipping-point so often moving and having to move. James says we have the power to help ourselves, but we may need the borrowed thought of the lost mother in order to release it.

And even if the need is hidden or rationalized within so-called normal life, the drama exists and continues beyond childhood. A drug addict known as Nemo, a nobody, dies alone and unmourned as if he had never been. 'If this forlorn man could have been pro-phetically seen lying here by the mother at whose breast he nestled, a little child...' writes Dickens. 'What an impossibility the vision would have seemed!' (*Bleak House*, 1853, chapter 11). That her child should grow up for it to come to that pass and end so. In fact it was almost impossible that this particular woman should ever know: she could never have foreseen it, and now is almost certainly long-dead. But *It*—the feeling of utmost loss in a human life, Bion's o— had to go somewhere, had to find a host for recognition some time, if not this one, with this particular nobody; has to come out and say something of what it is. The horizontal venture in William James is about the tenacious agnostic effort of going on forward 'in this dramatic shape of something sustaining a felt purpose against felt obstacles' (*A Pluralistic Universe*, appendix B)—and that despite the lack of clear and final goals. It has to go *on*, looking and feeling.

But so often, as we have seen James acknowledge, 'we don't come to our own': 'It is there but we don't get at it' ('The Energies of Men'). This present book is written within a series entitled *My Reading*; but when it comes to the unlocking of what is 'there' and what could be 'our own', '*My*' is what comes only after everything else, in retrospect, in what slows down into being a temporary rest within a second world. That non-dramatic world is not to be wholly believed in, only perched upon, waiting till the going-on again. What is to be believed in or at least risked is more blind and less secure. It is thinking at its best when the 'my' is only excitedly implicit again within whatever moves it, somehow, to somewhere. But the 'it' always has to be something that matters, matters to the implicit me absorbed in it. There is, says James, '*a plus*' that feeling provides, which is the message of personal significance (*VRE*, p. 346, lecture 18, 'Philosophy').

'It is there but we don't get at it.' Or we get it only through moments of crisis. I doubt it really because he never much respected systems, but James thought that he would have liked it if the discipline of psychology had been sufficiently advanced to have created 'a topographical survey'. He meant by that a comprehensive brain-map of all our capacities and potentials, 'made of the limits of human power in every conceivable direction, something like an opthalmologist's chart of the limits of the human field of vision'. Then we would better know how to get at ourselves. By means of that imagined map, there would be an 'inventory of the paths of access, or keys' ('The Energies of Men'), so that we could better access and use our deeper gifts.

But in the meantime, without such knowledge, there can be no more and no less than individual efforts and ventures 'to get at it'. This 'it' is, I repeat, the raw needy stuff of life that William James would fight for in any way and in any form he could. In an essay on 'The Moral Equivalent of War', revised from an earlier lecture near the very end of his life, he argued one last time for trying to keep the wild aggressive first instincts alive. Only he wanted to move their point, into the peaceable second world, so that, by mutual modification, those instincts did not go into physical acts of war, and that world wasn't a mere Chautauqua summer camp. He wanted to channel the energy and will of aggressive first instincts into fighting within civilization for what, still untamed and unnormalized, might make civilization worth having. As with Emerson, the true moment of culture was not created within culture but in the transition from the 'not yet' of the wild and the raw—the unformed and pre-professionalized, the personal and the rough and the chancy—into a better formulation and a better consolidation, always still in need of further revitalization.[10]

In that venture James says, in what feels like the closest he ever got to final words:

> Once more it is a case of *maybe*...For my part I do not know what the sweat and blood and tragedy of this life mean, if they mean any-thing short of this. If this life be not a real fight, in which something is eternally gained for the universe by success, it is no better than a game of private theatricals from which one may withdraw at will. But it feels like a real fight—as if there is were something really wild in the universe which we, with all our idealities and faithfulnesses, are needed to redeem; and first of all to redeem our own hearts from atheisms and fears. For such a half-wild, half-saved universe our nature is adapted.   ('Is Life Worth Living?')

It is not private theatricals. It *feels* like a real fight, and not just for one's self but for the sake of whatever, more largely, it tries to live within, allow, and make better. In whatever form fight must take, I find myself willing, says my James adorably, to try to do this work and to be this work.

So it is good that what William James offers is not a self-contained system of philosophy. Instead, it is nearer what D. H. Lawrence described in the final chapter of *Studies in Classic American Literature* (1924) as characteristic of the new American way, especially through Walt Whitman: a venture down 'the open road' in search of still unopened life. Its incompleteness means that his writing needs its readers for its development, as handed on in the human relay. His thought needs its human hosts and co-workers to feel it, to understand its implicitness, to put the spirit of it into practice, as far as is possible at any time, in diverse individual ways.

I'm too old now, says Strether at the end of Henry James's *The Ambassadors*, but for the future, for the next generation: 'Live all you can; it's a mistake not to.'

FURTHER READING

For further reading of James himself, there are the following selections:

The Heart of William James, ed. Robert Richardson (Harvard University Press, Cambridge Mass., 2012).

Pragmatism and Other Writings, ed. Giles Gunn (Penguin, London, 2000).

Selected Writings, ed. G. H. Bird (Everyman, J. M. Dent, London, 1995).

There are also two handsome volumes of his writings—1878–99; 1902–1910—published by the Library of America (New York, 1987, 1992).

There is a two-volume reprint of *The Principles of Psychology* (Dover Publications New York, 1950). *The Varieties of Religious Experience*, ed. Matthew Bradley, is published by World's Classics (Oxford University Press, 2012).

For biographies see R. B. Perry, *The Thought and Character of William James*, 2 vols (Little, Brown, and Company, Boston, 1935) and Robert D. Richardson, *William James in the Maelstrom of American Modernism* (Houghton Mifflin, New York, 2006).

Amongst the many writings on William James, I have found these particularly useful:

Jacques Barzun, *A Stroll with William James* (Harper and Row, New York, 1983).

Herwig Friedl, *Thinking in Search of a Language* (Bloomsbury, New York, 2019).

Bruce Mangan, 'Taking Phenomenology Seriously: The "Fringe" and Its Implications for Cognitive Research', *Consciousness and Cognition*, 1993, vol. 2, no. 2, 89–108.

James O. Pawelski, *The Dynamic Individualism of William James* (SUNY Press, Albany, New York, 2007).

Adam Phillips, 'The Conversions of William James', *Raritan*, summer 2017, vol. 37, no. 1, 21–39.

Ross Posnock, *The Trial of Curiosity: Henry James, William James and the Challenge of Modernity* (Oxford University Press, Oxford, 1991).

John Wild, *The Radical Empiricism of William James* (Doubleday, New York, 1969).

Other works that have helped the thinking in this book include:

Eugene T. Gendlin, *Focusing Oriented Psychotherapy* (Guilford Press, New York, 1996).

Brian G. Henning, William T. Myers, and Joseph D. John, eds, *Thinking with Whitehead and the American Pragmatists* (Lexington Books, Minneapolis, MN, 2015).

Vladimir Jankélévitch, *Henri Bergson*, tr. N. F. Schott (Duke University Press, Durham, 2015).

John Kaag, *American Philosophy: A Love Story* (Farrar, Straus and Giroux, New York, 2016).

Brian Massumi, *Parables for the Virtual* (Duke University Press, Durham, 2002).

Simon Palfrey, *Doing Shakespeare* (Arden Shakespeare, London, 2005).

Marilynne Robinson, *The Givenness of Things* (Virago, London, 2015).

Isabelle Stengers, *Thinking with Whitehead*, tr. Michael Chase (Harvard University Press, Cambridge, Mass., 2011).

NOTES

Chapter 1

1. Ralph Barton Perry, *The Thought and Character of William James*, briefer version (New York: George Braziller, 1954), p. 23, 17 March 1874 (hereafter cited as Perry).
2. *The Varieties of Religious Experience* (1902), edited by Matthew Bradley (Oxford: World's Classics) pp. 155–6, hereafter cited throughout as 'VRE'.
3. From William's introduction to his edition of *The Literary Remains of the Late Henry James* (Boston: Osgood, 1885), pp. 15–16.
4. *The Principles of Psychology* (1890), reproduced in 2 volumes, Dover, 1950, vol. 2, p. 298, chapter 21, 'The Perception of Reality'. I have used this as the most conveniently available authoritative edition, abbreviated as *PP*, citing also chapter and chapter title for ease of reference elsewhere.
5. Mary Douglas borrowed the term for her anthropological account of the artifice of social boundaries in her classic *Purity and Danger* (1966).
6. Letter to E. Tausch, 1909, and to Pauline Goldmark, 14 September 1901, quoted in Perry, pp. 365, 220.
7. John Jay Chapman, *Memories and Milestones* (New York: Moffat, Yard and Co., 1915), p. 26; hereafter cited as 'Chapman'.
8. See John F. Sears, 'William James, Henri Bergson, and the Poetics of Robert Frost', *The New England Quarterly*, September 1974, 48.3, 341–61, to which I am here indebted.
9. See Eugene Gendlin (2004), 'The New Phenomenology of Carrying Forward', *Continental Philosophy Review*, 37 (1), 127–51.

Chapter 2

1. John Jay Chapman, *Memories and Milestones* (New York: Moffat, Yard and Company, 1915) p. 22.

2. This is the so-called James-Lange theory of emotions, based first of all on physical reactions, formulated by William James in 'What Is an Emotion?', *Mind* (1884), 9, 188–205, and independently proposed by the Danish physiologist Carl Lange in a book-chapter on the mechanisms of emotion in 1885.

3. See *PP* 1, p. 371, chapter 10, 'The Consciousness of Self'.

4. In 'What Psychical Research Has Accomplished' and 'The Sentiment of Rationality'.

5. Victor Zuckerkandl, *Sound and Symbol*, translated by W. R. Trask (New York: Bollingen Foundation, Princeton University Press, 1969), pp. 208–9.

6. See Michael Witmore, *Culture of Accidents* (Stanford, California: Stanford University Press, 2001), especially introduction and chapter 1.

7. On the discontinuities hidden within the continuity, see 'On Some Hegelisms'.

8. John Keats, letter to Benjamin Bailey, 13 March 1818.

9. A. N. Whitehead, *Modes of Thought* (New York: Macmillan, 1938), p. vii.

10. Marina Warner in *The Observer*, 7 March 2021.

11. *Varieties of Religious Experience*, p. 380, lecture 20, 'Conclusions', *Pragmatism*, lecture 8 'Pragmatism and Religion', *A Pluralistic Universe*, lecture 6, 'Bergson and Intellectualism'.

12. Michael Polanyi, *Knowing and Being* (Routledge and Kegan Paul, 1969), p. 131. I first came to this on the recommendation of the literary critic F. R. Leavis in 1973, and though Polanyi believed that his theory of 'tacit knowledge' had significant differences from James's idea of the fringes of experience, it prefigured what James could do for me.

13. Bruce Mangan's doctoral thesis, *Meaning and the Structure of Consciousness* (University of California, 1991), pp. 12–13.

14. 'Answers to a Questionnaire' on religious beliefs in *William James: Writings 1902–1910* (Library of America, 1987) pp. 1184–5.

15. Letter to Mrs Henry Whitman, 7 June 1899, quoted in Ralph Barton Perry, *The Thought and Character of William James*, briefer version (New York: George Braziller, 1954), pp. 248–9.

16. *Letters*, 2 vols (Boston: Atlantic Monthly Press, 1920), vol. 2, pp. 277–8.

17. From Emerson's 'The Poet' in his second series of *Essays* (1844): 'all language is vehicular and transitive, and is good, as ferries and horses are, for conveyance, not as farms and houses are, for homestead'.

18. Eugene T. Gendlin, *Focusing* (1978) p. 134: http://previous.focusing.org/gendlin/docs/gol_2228.html

Chapter 3

1. F. D. Maurice, *Conscience* (London: Macmillan, 1868), p. 13.
2. *A Pluralistic Universe*, lecture 3, 'Some Metaphysical Problems Pragmatically Considered', lecture 7, 'The Continuity of Experience', and Appendix B, 'The Experience of Activity').
3. *PP* 1, p. 272, chapter 9, 'The Stream of Thought'.
4. Ralph Barton Perry, *The Thought and Character of William James*, briefer version (New York: George Braziller, 1954), p. 122: my italics, to show the force of the prepositions.
5. Les Murray, *The Paperbark Tree* (London: Carcanet, Minerva, 1993), p. 259.
6. See *Pragmatism*, the end of lecture 3, 'Some Metaphysical Problems Pragmatically Considered'.
7. In particular the chapter on 'Givenness' in her *The Givenness of Things* (Virago, 2015): 'I have been impressed for some time by American philosophical pragmatism' (p. 73)—particularly in James's *Varieties* with its acceptance of 'things in their complex and veiled givenness' (p. 80). To James, Robinson notes later, data is what is given, and what is given should be treated as a gift, as by grace ('Metaphysics', p. 189).
8. *PP* 1, pp. 239, 299–300, chapter 9, 'The Steam of Thought', chapter 10, 'The Consciousness of Self'.

Chapter 4

1. James knew Kierkegaard's formulation, twice quoting life is lived forwards but understood backwards, in lecture 6 of *Pragmatism* and 'Is Radical Empiricism Solipsistic?', *Essays in Radical Empiricism*.
2. *Manuscript Essays and Notes*, ed. F. Bowers and I.K. Skrupskelis, vol. 18 of *The Works of William James* (Harvard University Press, Cambridge, Mass. 1988), p. 8 (hereafter cited as 'MEN').
3. The Sentiment of Rationality', *Mind*, vol. 4, issue 15, July 1879, 341.
4. From a manuscript draft of the opening of *VRE* quoted in Ralph Barton Perry, *The Thought and Character of William James*, briefer version (New York: George Braziller, 1954), p. 258; 'How Two Minds Can Know One Thing' (1904), later incorporated into *Essays in Radical Empiricism* (1912).
5. *Talks to Teachers on Psychology* (1899), chapter 12, 'Memory' (hereafter cited as 'Talks').
6. Stanley Middleton, *An After-Dinner's Sleep* (Hutchinson, 1986), pp. 107, 174.

7. See Bruce Mangan, 'Taking Phenomenology Seriously: The "Fringe" and Its Implications for Cognitive Research', *Consciousness and Cognition*, 1993, vol. 2, 89 in particular, and throughout 89–108; to which I am gratefully indebted.

8. See also Brian Massumi, *Parables for the Virtual* (Duke University Press, Durham, 2002).

9. On the sensory/non-sensory distinction, and the economy of non-sensory markers working around the fringe of experience, see Bruce Mangan, 'Sensation's Ghost', *Psyche*, August 2001, 7 (18), https://www. researchgate.net/publication/247487522_Sensation%27s_ghost_The_ non-sensory_fringe_of_consciousness; also his 'Cognition, Fringe Consciousness, and the Legacy of William James' (2007), https://doi. org/10.1002/9780470751466.ch53.

10. 'Answers to a Questionnaire', in vol. 2 of the Library of America's edition of *William James, Writings 1902–1910* (New York: Library of America, 1987), p. 1184 (hereafter cited as AQ).

11. *The Letters of William James*, ed. Henry James (his eldest son) 1920, 2 vols (New York: Cosimo Classics, 2008), vol. 2, p. 62 (hereafter cited as *Letters*).

Chapter 5

1. *The Personal Notebooks of Thomas Hardy*, ed. Richard H. Taylor (London and Basingstoke: Macmillan, 1978), p. 89.

2. *The Life and Works of Thomas Hardy* (originally published under name of F. E. Hardy, 1928, 1930), ed. Michael Millgate (London and Basingstoke: Macmillan, 1984, pp. 153, 227). Hereafter cited as '*TH Life*'.

3. Marilynne Robinson, *What Are We Doing Here?* (Virago, 2018), p. 206.

4. John Jay Chapman, *Memories and Milestones* (New York: Moffat, Yard and Co, 1915), p. 22.

5. Catherine Charlwood, *Models of Memory: Cognition and Cultural Memory in the Poetry of Thomas Hardy and Robert Frost* (PhD thesis, 2017), pp. 22–3, http://wrap.warwick.ac.uk/91139.

6. Ralph Barton Perry, *The Thought and Character of William James*, briefer version (New York: George Braziller, 1954), p. 92 (hereafter cited as '*Perry*').

7. Mark Edmundson, *Self and Soul* (Cambridge, Mass.: Harvard University Press, 2015), pp. 257–8: 'At a certain point it will again become clear to young people that they have a choice in what they make of their lives. There are ideals of the Soul and there are desires of the Self, and young

people will once again have the chance to decide which they will pursue.'

8. Jacques Barzun, *A Stroll with William James* (New York: Harper and Row, 1983), p. 4.

9. William Edward Burghardt Du Bois, *The Souls of Black Folk* (Chicago: A. C. McClurg & Co., 1903, p. 3 (hereafter cited as '*The Souls of Black Folk*').

10. Derek A. Bardowell, *No Win Race* (Mudlark, 2019), p. 134.

11. Booker T. Washington (1856–1915) was a sort of non-Jamesian pragmatic alternative to Du Bois: the dominant leader of the Afro-American community, increasingly well-funded and media savvy, he was a skilled politician adept at compromise, rather than an aggressive opponent of continuing Southern segregation, and a promoter of entrepreneurial business with the emphasis on economics and technological education as the drivers of progress.

12. W. E. B. Du Bois, 'My Evolving Program for Negro Freedom', in *What the Negro Wants*, ed. Rayford Logan (Chapel Hill: University of North Carolina Press, 1944), pp. 57–8.

13. W. E. B. Du Bois, 'The Dilemma of the Negro', *American Mercury* (Oct. 1924): 179–85, p. 180, quoted by Ross Posnock, 'Going Astray, Going Forward: Du Boisian Pragmatism and Its Lineage', in *The Revival of Pragmatism: New Essays on Social Thought, Law, and Culture*, ed. Morris Dickstein (Durham, North Carolina: Duke, 1998), p. 182.

14. See Michael Bell, *Open Secrets* (Oxford: Oxford University Press, 2007), on the paradox of 'open secrets', at once half-revealed and half-concealed, and on the limits of the directly teachable, especially when the resonance of literary writing is designed to go beyond the transparently literal and explicit.

15. Joan Didion, 'Why I Write', Lithub: https://www.sevanoland.com/uploads/1/1/8/0/118081022/why_i_write_didion.pdf

16. From 'Your Last Drive', 'The Going', and 'Wessex Heights'.

17. Du Bois, *The Crisis Writings*, ed. Daniel Walden (Greenwich, Conn., Fawcett, 1972), p. 334.

Chapter 6

1. Respectively *War and Peace*, book 4, part 1, chapter 12; *Anna Karenina*, part 3, chapter 5; 'The Death of Ivan Ilyich', chapter 7.

2. See Michael Witmore, *Shakespearean Metaphysics* (London: Continuum, 2008) on the relation to process philosophy, especially Whitehead.

3. https://journal.wjsociety.org/wp-content/uploads/2014/11/PS.pdf.

4. My own interest is described in *Reading for Life* (Oxford: Oxford University Press, 2020), pp. 173–83 and is another of the reasons for my feeling an affinity with William James.

5. John Jay Chapman, *A Glance Toward Shakespeare* (Boston; Atlantic Monthly Press, 1922) p. 5.

6. I am indebted to Simon Palfrey and Tiffany Stern, *Shakespeare in Parts* (Oxford: Oxford University Press, 2007).

7. 'How Hard It Is to Keep from Being King When It's in You and in the Situation'.

8. Adapted from Simon Critchley, *How to Stop Living and Start Worrying* (Cambridge: Polity Press, 2010), p. 122.

9. Anna Freud, 'About Losing and Being Lost', in *The Writings of Anna Freud*, 8 vols (International Universities Press, 1976), vol. 4, pp. 302–16. I am indebted here to Adam Phillips.

10. Herwig Friedl, *Thinking in Search of a Language* (Bloomsbury, 2019), p. 201, with relation to another of James' students, Gertrude Stein on the need for 'beginning again and again'. He also quotes Emerson on it being better never to see a book than to let it intimidate its readers into believing there is nothing new left to think, stopping them from still seeking their own way.

INDEX

For the benefit of digital users, indexed terms that span two pages (e.g., 52–53) may, on occasion, appear on only one of those pages.